2-Basket Air Fryer Cookbook for Beginners:

Simple & Delicious Double Air Fryer Recipes for Your Dual Basket Air Fryer

Sophia Bexley

Introduction

Welcome to the flavorful world of the 2-Basket Air Fryer Cookbook, where culinary innovation meets the art of healthy cooking! This cookbook is your ultimate guide to mastering the versatility of a kitchen appliance that has taken the culinary landscape by storm. Designed to help you savor the best of both worlds, this cookbook is tailored to make the most of your 2-basket air fryer, unlocking a symphony of flavors while keeping a mindful eye on nutrition.

Within these pages, you'll embark on a culinary journey that transcends traditional frying methods. Whether you're a seasoned chef or a novice cook, you'll discover a delectable array of recipes that span cuisines, flavors, and dietary preferences. From perfectly crisp appetizers to succulent main courses, and even mouthwatering desserts, each recipe is meticulously crafted to ensure your 2-basket air fryer becomes your kitchen's culinary magician. Prepare to tantalize your taste buds, redefine your cooking routine, and embrace a healthier way of indulging in your favorite dishes with the 2-Basket Air Fryer Cookbook.

2-Basket Air Fryer

The 2-Basket Air Fryer is a testament to culinary innovation, redefining how we approach home cooking with its unparalleled versatility and efficiency. In a world where time is of the essence and flavor is paramount, this ingenious kitchen appliance offers a unique solution to whip up delectable dishes easily. Designed to cater to modern lifestyles, the 2-basket configuration doubles the convenience, allowing chefs of all levels to prepare two separate dishes simultaneously, each retaining its distinct taste and texture. Whether you're a seasoned chef experimenting with complex recipes or a busy parent aiming for quick yet nutritious meals, this appliance transcends mere cooking to become an essential tool for crafting culinary masterpieces that delight the palate.

Crafted to go beyond the limitations of conventional cooking methods, the 2-Basket Air Fryer employs cutting-edge technology that harnesses the power of hot air circulation to achieve crispy exteriors and tender interiors, all while using a fraction of the oil traditionally required. Its intuitive controls and diverse temperature settings empower users to customize cooking conditions for various recipes, from golden-brown fries to succulent chicken wings. As a beacon of efficiency, this appliance significantly reduces cooking times and contributes to healthier eating habits by minimizing oil usage. With its sleek design and thoughtful engineering, the 2-Basket Air Fryer adds a touch of sophistication to any kitchen countertop, promising a culinary journey where taste knows no bounds and creativity knows no limits.

Why Use a 2-Basket Air Fryer

The 2-Basket Air Fryer Cookbook offers many advantages that can significantly enhance your cooking experience and meal preparation, making it a valuable addition to your culinary arsenal.

Efficient Dual Cooking

With a 2-basket air fryer, you can simultaneously cook different foods at varying temperatures and times, optimizing cooking efficiency and reducing meal preparation time.

Time Savings

Prepare complete meals in one go by cooking proteins and sides simultaneously, eliminating the need for multiple cooking appliances or waiting for sequential cooking cycles.

Conserves Energy

Cooking multiple dishes together in the same appliance minimizes energy consumption compared to using multiple traditional cooking devices.

Enhanced Meal Planning

The cookbook provides recipes tailored for 2-basket air fryers, enabling you to effortlessly plan well-balanced meals that cater to diverse dietary preferences.

Space Efficiency

If kitchen counter space is a concern, the 2-basket air fryer's compact design lets you prepare multi-component meals without cluttering your countertop.

Consistent Results

With precise temperature and time controls for each basket, you'll achieve consistent cooking results across both baskets, avoiding overcooked or undercooked food.

Healthier Cooking

The air frying technique requires minimal oil, reducing unhealthy fat content in your meals while delivering crispy, delicious results.

Easy Cleanup:** Using fewer cooking appliances means fewer dishes to clean, and the air fryer's non-stick baskets make post-cooking cleanup a breeze.

Family-Friendly Meals

Prepare a variety of dishes suitable for everyone's preferences simultaneously, accommodating picky eaters and dietary restrictions with ease.

Entertaining Made Simple

When hosting gatherings, the 2-basket air fryer allows you to serve an assortment of appetizers, sides, and mains hot and ready all at once.

Reduced Odor and Smoke

Compared to traditional frying methods, the air fryer helps minimize cooking odors and smoke, ensuring a more pleasant cooking environment.

Budget-Friendly

Cooking two dishes in one appliance reduces energy consumption and overall meal costs, making the 2-basket air fryer an economical choice.

Adaptable Portions

Whether you're cooking for a small family or a larger gathering, the 2-basket air fryer allows you to adjust portion sizes conveniently while maintaining consistent cooking quality.

Incorporating the 2-Basket Air Fryer Cookbook into your culinary routine presents many advantages that can save you time, energy, and effort while enabling you to explore a wide array of delicious, healthy, and creatively prepared dishes.

Why use a 2-Basket Air Fryer Cookbook?

The 2-Basket Air Fryer Cookbook offers many compelling benefits and advantages that make it an indispensable kitchen companion for anyone seeking culinary excellence and convenience. Here are 15 detailed reasons why using this cookbook can significantly enhance your cooking experience:

1) Diverse Recipe Selection

The cookbook boasts a wide variety of recipes, from appetizers to desserts, ensuring you can effortlessly create complete meals using your 2-basket air fryer. This eliminates the need for multiple appliances and simplifies meal planning.

2) Time Efficiency

With clear instructions and optimized cooking times, the cookbook helps you prepare meals more quickly than traditional cooking methods. This is especially beneficial for busy individuals looking to put nutritious and delicious meals on the table in minimal time.

3) Healthier Cooking

The 2-basket air fryer minimizes the need for excessive oil, leading to healthier meals. This cookbook maximizes this advantage by providing recipes emphasizing air frying and reducing unhealthy fats while retaining mouthwatering flavors and textures.

4) Nutritional Information

Each recipe is accompanied by detailed nutritional information, enabling you to make informed choices about your dietary intake. This is especially valuable for those with specific health goals or dietary restrictions.

5) Temperature and Timing Accuracy

The cookbook's precise guidelines for temperature settings and cooking times ensure consistent and perfectly cooked dishes every time, minimizing the risk of overcooking or undercooking.

6) Ingredient Adaptability

Whether you're cooking for a family with diverse tastes or accommodating allergies, the cookbook's adaptable recipes allow for easy ingredient substitutions while still achieving scrumptious results.

7) Effortless Cleanup

Cooking with the 2-basket air fryer inherently reduces mess, and the cookbook's emphasis on simplified recipes and cooking techniques further streamlines the cleanup process.

8) Crispy Texture Mastery

Achieving a crispy exterior while retaining moisture within food can be challenging. The cookbook provides expert tips and techniques to help you achieve that perfect texture in various dishes.

9) Cost-Effective Cooking

By requiring less oil and energy than traditional frying methods, the cookbook helps you save on grocery costs and utility bills over time.

10)   Exploration of Cuisines

With recipes spanning various global cuisines, the cookbook encourages culinary exploration, allowing you to create international dishes with ease and authenticity.

11) Portion Control Assistance

The cookbook's serving size recommendations and nutritional information empower you to practice portion control more effectively, contributing to weight management and balanced eating habits.

12)   Impressive Entertaining

Whether you're hosting a casual gathering or a special occasion, the cookbook equips you with crowd-pleasing recipes that showcase your culinary prowess without the stress of elaborate cooking methods.

13)   Beginner-Friendly Approach

Even if you're new to cooking or air frying, the cookbook's step-by-step instructions and clear explanations ensure a smooth and enjoyable cooking experience.

14)   Waste Reduction

With well-planned recipes, the cookbook minimizes food waste by guiding you on using ingredients efficiently and creatively.

15)   Family Involvement

Cooking with a 2-basket air fryer can be a fun and educational activity for the whole family. The cookbook's user-friendly instructions make it easy to involve children in the kitchen, fostering valuable life skills and positive family interactions.

How to use the cookbook

The 2-Basket Air Fryer Cookbook is designed to simplify your cooking experience and maximize the potential of your air fryer. It offers various recipes categorized into breakfast, lunch, seafood and fish, red meat, poultry, side dishes, snacks, vegetables, and desserts. With its user-friendly approach, you can confidently embark on a culinary journey that balances health, taste, and convenience.

Getting Started

Before diving into the recipes, familiarize yourself with your 2-basket air fryer's features, controls, and settings. Review the cookbook's introductory section that provides essential tips on preheating, temperature adjustment, and proper placement of baskets to ensure optimal cooking results.

Breakfast Delights

Start your day with a selection of hearty breakfast recipes. From crispy hash browns to cinnamon French toast sticks, the cookbook guides you through preparing morning favorites that are both nutritious and satisfying. Tips on achieving the perfect golden-brown texture while cooking breakfast foods are provided, ensuring your meals are visually appealing and delicious.

Wholesome Lunch Choices

The lunch section offers a variety of recipes ranging from sandwiches and wraps to salads and grain bowls. Discover creative ways to incorporate lean proteins, vibrant vegetables, and flavorful sauces into your midday meals. The cookbook's instructions on multitasking within the two baskets enable you to prepare a complete lunch in one cooking cycle efficiently.

Seafood and Fish Extravaganza

For seafood enthusiasts, this section provides step-by-step guidance on preparing succulent shrimp, flaky fish fillets, and other aquatic delights. The cookbook highlights the air fryer's ability to cook seafood perfectly, sealing in moisture while creating a delectably crisp exterior.

Savoring Red Meat Dishes

Indulge in the richness of red meat with recipes that cover everything from juicy burgers to tender steak cuts. The cookbook's temperature and timing recommendations ensure that your meat dishes are cooked to your preferred level of doneness while minimizing excess fat.

Perfectly Cooked Poultry

Explore a range of poultry recipes, from crispy chicken wings to succulent turkey burgers. The cookbook guides you through the art of achieving crispy skin and juicy meat, utilizing the dual baskets to cook different poultry cuts efficiently.

Delectable Side Dishes

Complement your main courses with an array of side dish options. From roasted vegetables to crispy sweet potato fries, these recipes showcase the versatility of your 2-basket air fryer. Learn how to utilize both baskets effectively for a well-rounded meal.

Irresistible Snacks

Discover quick and savory snack options perfect for on-the-go munching or movie nights. The cookbook's snack recipes utilize the air fryer's speed and efficiency to create crispy treats without the excess oil typically associated with traditional frying methods.

Wholesome Vegetable Creations

Elevate your vegetable game with dishes that retain their natural flavors and textures. The cookbook's vegetable recipes offer guidance on achieving the ideal balance between a tender interior and a crispy exterior, making each bite a delightful experience.

Divine Desserts

Round off your meals with a selection of sweet treats. From fruit crisps to churros, the cookbook's dessert section showcases how the air fryer can create delectable desserts that are indulgent and lower in fat compared to traditional baking.

Utilizing the Cookbook's Layout

The cookbook's layout is designed for ease of use. Each recipe includes a list of ingredients, step-by-step instructions, and suggested cooking times. Pay attention to cooking variations and tips provided by the authors to enhance your cooking skills and adapt recipes to your taste preferences.

Customizing Recipes

Feel free to customize recipes to suit your dietary needs and preferences. The cookbook encourages ingredient substitutions while maintaining the essence of each dish. Explore different seasoning options, sauces, and toppings to make each recipe your own.

Mastering Dual-Basket Cooking

The cookbook's expertise lies in utilizing the 2-basket air fryer's capabilities. Embrace the practice of multitasking, cooking proteins and sides simultaneously in different baskets, and achieving harmonious flavors within a single cooking cycle.

Embracing the Culinary Journey

Using the 2-Basket Air Fryer Cookbook is not just about cooking; it's about expanding your culinary horizons. Experiment with recipes, adapt techniques and share your newfound skills with family and friends. The cookbook encourages you to enjoy cooking with your 2-basket air fryer, exploring a world of flavors and textures while maintaining a healthy and efficient kitchen routine.

Using the 2-Basket Air Fryer

The 2-Basket Air Fryer is a versatile kitchen appliance that cooks various dishes using hot air circulation. This detailed guide will walk you through the different parts of the air fryer, its settings, and how to make the most of its functions.

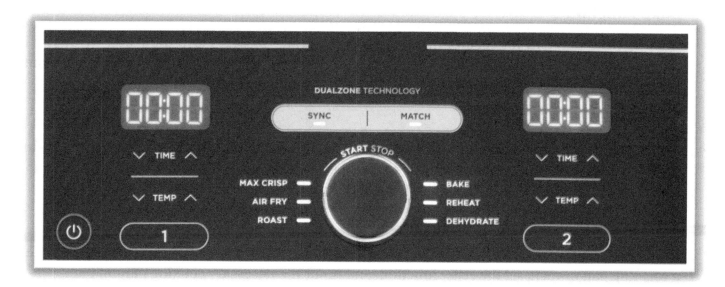

Parts of the 2-Basket Air Fryer:

Control Panel

The control panel is where you select cooking settings, adjust temperatures, and set cooking times. It typically features a digital display for easy monitoring.

Cooking Baskets

The air fryer has two cooking baskets, allowing you to cook different dishes simultaneously. These baskets have a non-stick coating to prevent sticking and simplify cleanup.

Heating Element and Fan

The heating element generates hot air, while the fan circulates the air throughout the cooking chamber. This combination results in even cooking and a crispy texture.

Drip Tray

The drip tray collects excess oil or drippings beneath the cooking baskets, keeping the appliance and your food cleaner.

Accessories

Some models might come with additional accessories such as skewers, racks, or baking pans, expanding the range of dishes you can prepare.

Cooking Settings and Functions:

Fry Function

This setting mimics deep frying without the need for excessive oil. It's perfect for creating crispy favorites like French fries, chicken tenders, or fried vegetables. Preheat the air fryer, place the food in the baskets, and select the fry function, desired temperature, and cooking time.

Bake Function

Use the bake function for recipes like cakes, muffins, and pizzas. Place the batter or dough in appropriate baking pans or trays, set the bake function, and adjust temperature and time accordingly.

Grill Function

Achieve grill-like char marks and flavors using the grill function. This is excellent for cooking meats, fish, or even grilled sandwiches. Preheat the air fryer, place the food on the grill rack, and choose the grill function with the appropriate settings.

Roast Function

The roast function is ideal for larger cuts of meat, whole chickens, or even roasted vegetables. Use a roasting pan or rack, set the roast function, and input the necessary cooking parameters.

Dehydrate Function

The dehydrate function is handy for preserving fruits, making jerky, or drying herbs. Spread thinly sliced items on the racks, select the dehydrate function, and set the temperature and time for thorough drying.

Usage Steps:

Preparation

Prep your ingredients according to the recipe. Some dishes might require marinating, seasoning, or coating with a light layer of oil.

Preheating

Preheat the air fryer to the recommended temperature for the chosen function. Preheating ensures even cooking and a crispy texture.

Loading the Baskets

Place the prepared food in the cooking baskets, making sure not to overcrowd them. Adequate spacing allows hot air to circulate freely.

Setting Parameters

Use the control panel to select the desired function (fry, bake, grill, roast, or dehydrate), set the temperature, and input the cooking time. Refer to the cookbook or recipe guidelines for specific settings.

Cooking

Once parameters are set, start the cooking process. The air fryer will automatically begin circulating hot air to cook the food evenly.

Monitoring

Periodically check the food's progress through the transparent lid or by opening the baskets. This is a good time to toss or flip the food for uniform cooking.

Adjusting Settings

If needed, you can adjust the temperature or cooking time during the process based on how the food is cooking.

Completion

Once the cooking cycle is complete, carefully remove the baskets using oven mitts or tongs. Place the cooked food on a plate and let it cool slightly before serving.

Breakfast Recipes

Bacon & Spinach Cups + Cloud Eggs

Cooking period: 19 mins. | Serving portions: 3

Cloud Eggs: Per Serving: Calories 129, Carbs 13g, Fat 5.2g, Protein 7.5g

Bacon & Spinach Cups: Per Serving: Calories 442, Carbs 2.3g, Fat 34.5g, Protein 26.9g

For the Bacon & Spinach Cups	For the Cloud Eggs:
<ul><li>Eggs – 3</li><li>Bacon slices – 6, cut up</li><li>Fresh spinach – 2 C.</li><li>Heavy cream – 1/3 C.</li><li>Parmesan cheese – 3 tbsp. grated</li><li>Salt and powdered black pepper, as desired</li></ul>	<ul><li>Eggs – 3, whites and yolks separated</li><li>Salt and powdered black pepper, as desired</li><li>Bread slices – 3, toasted</li></ul>

Method of Cooking:

1. For the bacon and spinach cups, sizzle an anti-sticking wok on the burner at medium-high heat.
2. Cook the bacon for around 6-8 minutes. Stir in the spinach. Cook for around 2-3 minutes.
3. Mix in the heavy cream and Parmesan cheese. Cook for around 2-3 minutes.
4. Take it off the burner and put it aside to cool slightly.
5. To turn on the 2-Basket Air Fryer, press "Power". Then press "Start/Pause" to start cooking.
6. Press "Zone 1" and choose "Air Fry".
7. Press "Temp" to adjust to 350°F and then press "Time" for 5 minutes to preheat.
8. Crack 1 egg 1 in each of 6 greased ramekins and top with bacon mixture.
9. After preheating, lay the ramekins in the "Zone 1" basket.
10. Slide the basket into the Air Fryer and set the time for 5 minutes
11. Meanwhile, press "Zone 2" for the cloud eggs and choose "Air Broil". Set the time for 5 minutes to preheat.
12. Put the egg white, salt, and pepper into a basin and whisk to form stiff peaks.
13. Lay out baking paper into a baking pan. With a large-sized spoon, lay out egg whites in the baking pan.
14. Carefully make a pocket in the center of each egg white circle.
15. After preheating, lay the baking pan into the "Zone 2" basket.
16. Slide the basket into the Air Fryer and press "Time" to adjust for 7 minutes.
17. After 5 minutes of cooking, put 1 egg yolk into each egg white pocket.
18. After cooking time is finished, press "Start/Pause" to stop cooking.
19. Take out the ramekins and baking pan from the Air Fryer.
20. Sprinkle the top of each cup with salt and pepper, and enjoy hot.
21. Enjoy cloud eggs moderately hot alongside the bread slices.

Salmon Quiche + Savory French Toast

Cooking period: 20 mins. | Serving portions: 2

Salmon Quiche: Per Serving: Calories 592, Carbs 33.8g, Fat 10g, Protein 27.2g

Savory French Toasts: Per Serving: Calories 110, Carbs 20.4g, Fat 1.6g, Protein 4.8g

For the Salmon Quiche:	**For the Savory French Toast:**
• Salmon fillet – 5½ oz. cut up • Salt and powdered black pepper, as desired • Lemon juice – ½ tbsp. • Egg yolk – 1 • Chilled butter – 3½ tbsp. • All-purpose flour – 2/3 C. • Cold water – 1 tbsp. • Eggs – 2 • Whipping cream – 3 tbsp. • Scallion – 1, cut up.	• Chickpea flour – ¼ C. • Onion – 3 tbsp. finely cut up • Green chili – 2 tsp. seeds removed and finely cut up • Red chili powder – ½ tsp. • Powdered turmeric – ¼ tsp. • Powdered cumin – ¼ tsp. • Salt, as desired • Water, as needed • Bread slices – 4

Method of Cooking:

1. Put salmon, salt, pepper, and lemon juice into a basin for the quiche and stir to incorporate. Put it aside.
2. Put the egg yolk, butter, flour, and water into another basin and mix to form a dough.
3. Place the dough onto a floured smooth counter and roll into about 7-inch round.
4. Lay the dough into a quiche pan and press firmly in the bottom and along the edges. Then, trim the excess edges.
5. Put the egg, cream, salt, and pepper into a small basin and whisk to incorporate thoroughly.
6. Place the cream mixture over the crust and top with the cut-up salmon, followed by the scallion.
7. For quiche: to turn on the 2-Basket Air Fryer, press "Power". Then press "Start/Pause" to start cooking.
8. Press "Zone 1" and choose "Air Fry".
9. Press "Temp" to adjust to 355ºF and then press "Time" for 5 minutes to preheat.
10. After preheating, lay out the quiche pan into the "Zone 1" basket.
11. Slide the basket into the Air Fryer and press "Time" to adjust for 20 minutes.
12. Meanwhile, spray the basket of "Zone 2" for the French toast. Press "Zone 2" and choose "Air Fry". Press "Temp" to adjust at 390ºF and then press "Time" for 5 minutes to preheat.
13. Put chickpea flour and remnant ingredients except for bread slices into a large-sized basin and stir to form a thick mixture. Spread the mixture over both sides of each bread slice with a spoon.
14. After preheating, lay the bread slices in the "Zone 2" basket.
15. Slide the basket into the Air Fryer and press "Time" to adjust for 5 minutes.
16. While cooking, change the side of the bread slices once halfway through.
17. After cooking time is finished, press "Start/Pause" to stop cooking.
18. Take out the baking pan and bread slices from Air Fryer. Enjoy moderately hot.

Ham Casserole + Cheese Omelet

Cooking period: 12 mins. | Serving portions: 2

Ham Casserole: Per Serving: Calories 306, Carbs 2.7g, Fat 23.8g, Protein 20.5g

Cheese Omelet: Per Serving: Calories 202, Carbs 1.8g, Fat 15.1g, Protein 14.8g

For the Ham Casserole:	For the Cheese Omelet:
<ul><li>Large-sized eggs – 4, divided</li><li>Salt and powdered black pepper, as desired</li><li>Heavy cream – 2 tbsp.</li><li>Unsalted butter – 2 tsp. softened</li><li>Ham 2 oz. – slivered thinly</li><li>Paprika – 1/8 tsp.</li><li>Parmesan cheese – 3 tbsp. finely grated</li><li>Fresh chives – 2 tsp. finely cut up</li></ul>	<ul><li>Eggs – 4</li><li>Cream – ¼ C.</li><li>Salt and powdered black pepper, as desired</li><li>Cheddar cheese – ¼ C. grated</li></ul>

Method of Cooking:

1. For the casserole: to turn on the 2-Basket Air Fryer, press "Power". Then press "Start/Pause" to start cooking.
2. Press "Zone 1" and choose "Air Fry".
3. Press "Temp" to adjust at 320°F and then press "Time" for 5 minutes to preheat.
4. Put 1 egg, salt, pepper, and cream into a basin and whisk to form a smooth mixture.
5. In the bottom of a pie pan, spread the butter.
6. Place the ham slices over the butter and top with the egg mixture.
7. Carefully crack remnant eggs on top and sprinkle with paprika, salt, and pepper.
8. Top with cheese and chives.
9. After preheating, lay the pan dish in the "Zone 1" basket.
10. Slide the basket into the Air Fryer and press "Time" to adjust for 12 minutes.
11. Meanwhile, press "Zone 2" for the omelet and choose "Air Fry".
12. Press "Temp" to adjust to 350°F and then press "Time" for 5 minutes to preheat.
13. Put the eggs, cream, salt, and pepper into a basin and whisk to incorporate thoroughly.
14. Place the egg mixture into a lightly greased small-sized baking pan.
15. After preheating, lay the baking pan into the "Zone 2" basket.
16. Slide the basket into the Air Fryer and press "Time" to adjust for 8 minutes.
17. After 4 minutes of cooking, sprinkle the cheese on the omelet.
18. After cooking time is finished, press "Start/Pause" to stop cooking.
19. Take out both pans from the Air Fryer.
20. Cut the omelet and quiche into serving portions and enjoy hot.

Banana Muffin + Eggs with Chicken & Kale

Cooking period: 20 mins. | Serving portions: 4

Eggs with Chicken & Kale: Per Serving: Calories 237, Carbs 12.5g, Fat 9.7g, Protein 25.6g

Banana Muffins: Per Serving: Calories 200, Carbs 19.6g, Fat 13.1g, Protein 2.2g

For the Eggs with Chicken & Kale:	For the Banana Muffins:
<ul><li>Olive oil – 1 tbsp.</li><li>Fresh baby kale – 1 lb. cut up</li><li>Eggs – 4</li><li>Cooked chicken – 8 oz. finely cut up</li><li>Milk – 4 tsp.</li><li>Salt and powdered black pepper, as desired</li><li>Dried rosemary – ¼ tsp.</li></ul>	<ul><li>Oats – ¼ C.</li><li>Refined flour – ¼ C.</li><li>Baking powder – ½ tsp.</li><li>Powdered sugar – ¼ C.</li><li>Unsalted butter – ¼ C. softened</li><li>Banana – ¼ C. peel removed and mashed</li><li>Milk – 1 tsp.</li><li>Walnuts – 1 tbsp. cut up</li></ul>

Method of Cooking:

1. For the eggs with chicken & kale, sizzle oil into a wok on a burner at around medium heat.
2. Cook the kale for around 3-4 minutes. Take off the burner and put it aside to cool slightly.
3. To turn on the 2-Basket Air Fryer, press "Power". Then press "Start/Pause" to start cooking.
4. Press "Zone 1" and choose "Air Fry".
5. Press "Temp" to adjust at 355°F and then press "Time" for 5 minutes to preheat.
6. Divide the cooked kale into 4 greased ramekins, followed by the chicken.
7. Crack 1 egg 1 into each ramekin and drizzle with milk. Sprinkle with salt, pepper, and rosemary.
8. After preheating, lay the ramekins in the "Zone 1" basket.
9. Slide the basket into the Air Fryer and press "Time" to adjust for 20 minutes.
10. Meanwhile, put oats, flour, and baking powder into a basin for the muffins and mix to incorporate.
11. Put the sugar and butter into another basin and whisk to form a creamy mixture.
12. Put in banana and vanilla extract and whisk to incorporate thoroughly
13. Put flour mixture and milk in the banana mixture and stir until just incorporated.
14. Lightly stir in the walnuts.
15. Place the mixture into 4 greased silicone muffin molds. Press "Zone 2" and choose "Air Fry".
16. Press "Temp" to adjust at 320°F and then press "Time" for 5 minutes to preheat.
17. After preheating, lay the muffin molds into the "Zone 2" basket.
18. Slide the basket into the Air Fryer and press "Time" to adjust for 10 minutes.
19. After cooking time is finished, press "Start/Pause" to stop cooking.
20. Take out the ramekins and muffin molds from the Air Fryer.
21. Place the muffin molds onto a counter to cool for around 10 minutes.
22. Carefully remove the muffins from the molds and move them onto a platter to cool thoroughly before enjoying.

Zucchini & Apple Bread + Nuts & Seeds Granola

Cooking period: 30 mins. | Serving portions: 8

Zucchini & Apple Bread: Per Serving: Calories 225, Carbs 24g, Fat 13.3g, Protein 3.9g

Nuts & Seeds Granola: Per Serving: Calories 302, Carbs 35.1g, Fat 16.1g, Protein 6.9g

For the Zucchini & Apple Bread:	For the Nuts & Seeds Granola:
For the Bread: • All-purpose flour – 1 C. • Baking powder – ¾ tsp. • Baking soda – ¼ tsp. • Powdered cinnamon – 1¼ tsp. • Salt – ¼ tsp. • Vegetable oil – 1/3 C. • White sugar – 1/3 C. • Egg – 1 • Vanilla extract – 1 tsp. • Zucchini – ½ C. shredded • Apple – ½ C. cored and shredded • Walnuts – 5 tbsp. cut up **For the Topping:** • Walnuts – 1 tbsp. cut up • Brown sugar – 2 tsp. • Powdered cinnamon – ¼ tsp.	• Canola oil – 1/3 C. • Maple syrup – ¼ C. • Honey – 2 tbsp. • Vanilla extract – ½ tsp. • Rolled oats – 2 C. • Wheat germ – ½ C. toasted • Dried cherries – ¼ C. • Dried blueberries – ¼ C. • Dried cranberries – 2 tbsp. • Sunflower seeds – 2 tbsp. • Pumpkin seeds – 2 tbsp. shelled • Flaxseeds – 1 tbsp. • Pecans – 2 tbsp. cut up • Hazelnuts – 2 tbsp. cut up • Almonds – 2 tbsp. cut up • Walnuts – 2 tbsp. cut up • Powdered cinnamon – ½ tsp.

Method of Cooking:

1. For the bread: put flour, baking powder, baking soda, cinnamon, and salt into a basin and stir to incorporate.
2. Put the oil, sugar, egg, and vanilla extract into another large-sized bowl and mix to incorporate thoroughly.
3. Put in flour mixture and stir until just incorporated
4. Lightly mix in the zucchini, apple, and walnuts.
5. For the topping: Put walnuts and remnant ingredients into a small-sized basin and whisk to incorporate thoroughly.
6. Place the mixture into a lightly greased loaf pan and sprinkle with the topping mixture.
7. To turn on the 2-Basket Air Fryer, press "Power".
8. Then press "Start/Pause" to start cooking.
9. Press "Zone 1" and choose "Air Fry".

10. Press "Temp" to adjust at 325°F and then press "Time" for 5 minutes to preheat.
11. After preheating, lay the loaf pan into the "Zone 1" basket.
12. Slide the basket into the Air Fryer and press "Time" to adjust for 30 minutes.
13. Meanwhile, put the oil and maple syrup into a small basin for the granola and stir to incorporate thoroughly.
14. Put remnant ingredients into a large-sized basin and stir to incorporate thoroughly.
15. Put in the oil mixture and stir to incorporate thoroughly.
16. Place the mixture into the baking pan and spread into an even layer.
17. Press "Zone 2" and choose "Air Fry".
18. Press "Temp" to adjust at 350°F and then press "Time" for 5 minutes to preheat.
19. After preheating, lay the baking pan into the "Zone 2" basket.
20. Slide the basket into the Air Fryer and press "Time" to adjust for 15 minutes.
21. While cooking, stir the granola after every 5 minutes.
22. After cooking time is finished, press "Start/Pause" to stop cooking.   Take off both pans from the Air Fryer.
23. Put the granola aside to cool thoroughly before enjoying it.
24. Place the loaf pan onto a counter to cool for around 10 minutes.
25. Remove the bread from the pan onto a platter to cool thoroughly.
26. Cut the bread into serving portions and enjoy.

Lunch Recipes

Scallops with Spinach + Tofu with Cauliflower

Cooking period: 15 mins. Serving portions: 2

Scallops with Spinach: Per Serving: Calories 309, Carbs 12.3g, Fat 18.8g, Protein 26.4g

Tofu with Cauliflower: Per Serving: Calories 170, Carbs 8.3g, Fat 11.6g, Protein 11.9 g

For the Scallops with Spinach:	**For the Tofu with Cauliflower:**
<ul><li>Heavy whipping cream – ¾ C.</li><li>Tomato paste – 1 tbsp.</li><li>Garlic – 1 tsp. finely cut up</li><li>Fresh basil – 1 tbsp. choppy</li><li>Salt and powdered black pepper, as desired</li><li>Jumbo sea scallops – 8</li><li>Olive oil baking spray</li><li>Frozen spinach – – 1 (12-oz.) package, thawed and drained</li></ul>	<ul><li>Firm tofu – ½ (14-oz.) block, pressed and cubed</li><li>Small-sized head cauliflower – ½, cut into florets</li><li>Canola oil – 1 tbsp.</li><li>Nutritional yeast – 1 tbsp.</li><li>Dried parsley – ¼ tsp.</li><li>Powdered turmeric – 1 tsp.</li><li>Paprika – ¼ tsp.</li><li>Salt and powdered black pepper, as desired</li></ul>

Method of Cooking:

1. Put the cream, tomato paste, garlic, basil, salt, and pepper into a basin and stir to incorporate thoroughly.
2. Spray each scallop with baking spray and sprinkle with salt and pepper.
3. In the bottom of a baking pan, put the spinach.
4. Lay out scallops over spinach and top with the cream mixture.
5. To turn on the 2-Basket Air Fryer, press "Power". Then press "Start/Pause" to start cooking.
6. Spray the basket of "Zone 1". Press "Zone 1" and choose "Air Fry".
7. Press "Temp" to adjust at 350⁰F and then press "Time" for 5 minutes to preheat.
8. After preheating, lay the baking pan into the "Zone 1" basket.
9. Slide the basket into the Air Fryer and press "Time" to adjust for 10 minutes.
10. Meanwhile, for the tofu, put tofu, cauliflower, and remnant ingredients into a basin and stir to incorporate.
11. Spray the basket of "Zone 2". Press "Zone 2" and choose "Air Fry".
12. Press "Temp" to adjust at 390⁰F and then press "Time" for 5 minutes to preheat.
13. After preheating, lay out the tofu mixture in the "Zone 2" basket.
14. Slide the basket into the Air Fryer and press "Time" to adjust for 15 minutes.
15. Change the side of tofu cubes once halfway through.
16. After cooking time is finished, press "Start/Pause" to stop cooking.
17. Take out the baking pans of scallop mixture and tofu mixture from the Air Fryer. Enjoy immediately.

Pork Stuffed Bell Peppers + Spiced Shrimp

Cooking period: 1 hr. 10 mins. | Serving portions: 4 |

Pork Stuffed Bell Peppers: Per Serving: Calories 580, Carbs 96.4g, Fat 7.1g, Protein 30.3g

Spiced Shrimp: Per Serving: Calories 294, Carbs 2.9g, Fat 13.5g, Protein 38.9g

For the Pork Stuffed Bell Peppers:	**For the Spiced Shrimp:**
<ul><li>Medium-sized bell peppers – 4</li><li>Ground pork – 2/3 lb.</li><li>Cooked white rice – 2 C.</li><li>Marinara sauce – 1½ C. divided</li><li>Worcestershire sauce – 1 tsp.</li><li>Italian seasoning – 1 tsp.</li><li>Salt and powdered black pepper, as desired</li><li>Mozzarella cheese – ½ C. shredded</li></ul>	<ul><li>Shrimp – 1½ lb. peeled and deveined</li><li>Olive oil – 3 tbsp.</li><li>Old bay seasoning – 1 tsp.</li><li>Cayenne pepper powder – ½ tsp.</li><li>Paprika – ½ tsp.</li><li>Salt, as desired</li></ul>

Method of Cooking:

1. For the stuffed bell peppers, cut the tops from the bell peppers and then carefully remove the seeds.
2. Sizzle a large-sized wok on a burner at around medium heat.
3. Cook the pork for around 6-8 minutes.
4. Put in rice, ¾ C. of marinara sauce, Worcestershire sauce, Italian seasoning, salt, and pepper, and mix to incorporate.
5. Take off from burner.
6. Carefully stuff each bell pepper with the pork mixture and top each with remnant sauce.
7. To turn on the 2-Basket Air Fryer, press "Power".
8. Then press "Start/Pause" to start cooking.
9. Spray the basket of "Zone 1". Press "Zone 1" and choose "Bake".
10. Press "Temp" to adjust at 350°F and then press "Time" for 5 minutes to preheat.
11. After preheating, lay the bell peppers in the "Zone 1" basket.
12. Slide the basket into the Air Fryer and press "Time" to adjust for 60 minutes.
13. After 50 minutes of cooking, top each bell pepper with cheese.
14. Meanwhile, for the shrimp, put shrimp and remnant ingredients into a large-sized basin and stir to incorporate.
15. Spray the basket of "Zone 2".
16. Press "Zone 2" and choose "Air Fry".
17. Press "Temp" to adjust at 390°F and then press "Time" for 5 minutes to preheat.
18. After preheating, lay the shrimp in the "Zone 2" basket.
19. Slide the basket into the Air Fryer and press "Time" to adjust for 5 minutes.
20. After cooking time is finished, press "Start/Pause" to stop cooking.
21. Take out the bell peppers and shrimp from Air Fryer and Enjoy moderately hot.

Tofu in Orange Sauce + Beef Enchiladas

Cooking period: 10 mins. Serving portions: 4

Tofu in Orange Sauce: Per Serving: Calories 147, Carbs 12.7g, Fat 6.7g, Protein 12.1g

Beef Enchiladas: Per Serving: Calories 436, Carbs 34.4g, Fat 371g, Protein 52.8g

For the Tofu in Orange Sauce:	For the Beef Enchiladas:
For the Tofu:	• Flour tortillas – – 2 (12-inch)
	• Cooked beef – 2 C. shredded and divided
• Extra-firm tofu – 1 lb. pressed and cubed	• Mexican cheese blend – 10 oz. shredded and divided
• Cornstarch – 1 tbsp.	• Large-sized tomatoes – 2, cut up and divided
• Tamari – 1 tbsp.	• Corn tostadas – 2, divided
For the Sauce:	
• Water – ½ C.	
• Orange juice – 1/3 C.	
• Maple syrup – 1 tbsp.	
• Orange zest – 1 tsp. grated	
• Garlic – 1 tsp. finely cut up	
• Fresh ginger – 1 tsp. finely cut up	
• Cornstarch – 2 tsp.	
• Red pepper flakes – ¼ tsp. crushed	

Method of Cooking:

1. For the tofu: put the tofu, cornstarch, and tamari into a basin and toss to incorporate thoroughly.
2. Put the tofu aside to marinate for at least 15 minutes.
3. To turn on the 2-Basket Air Fryer, press "Power".
4. Then press "Start/Pause" to start cooking.
5. Spray the basket of "Zone 1".
6. Press "Zone 1" and choose "Air Fry".
7. Press "Temp" to adjust to 390°F and then press "Time" for 5 minutes to preheat.
8. After preheating, lay the tofu cubes in the "Zone 1" basket.
9. Slide the basket into the Air Fryer and press "Time" to adjust for 10 minutes.
10. Change the side of tofu cubes once halfway through.
11. Meanwhile, for the sauce, put water and remnant ingredients in a small-sized saucepan on the burner at around medium-high heat.
12. Cook the mixture until boiling, stirring all the time.
13. Take off the burner and pour the sauce into a large-sized basin.
14. Meanwhile, lay the tortillas on a clean, smooth counter for the enchiladas.

15. Place about ½ C. of shredded beef onto the center of the tortilla, followed by 2 oz. of the cheese, half of the tomatoes, and 1 tostada.
16. Repeat the layers once and finally top with remnant 1 oz. of cheese.
17. Gently fold the tortilla over the filling in 4 layers.
18. Cover the enchilada's center opening with a broken piece of tostada to secure the filling.
19. Spray the basket of "Zone 2".
20. Press "Zone 2" and choose "Air Fry".
21. Press "Temp" to adjust at 380°F and then press "Time" for 5 minutes to preheat.
22. After preheating, lay out the enchilada into the "Zone 2" basket, seam-side down.
23. Slide the basket into the Air Fryer and press "Time" to adjust for 8 minutes.
24. After cooking time is finished, press "Start/Pause" to stop cooking.
25. Take out the tofu cubes and enchiladas from the Air Fryer.
26. Place the tofu into the basin with sauce and lightly stir to incorporate.
27. Enjoy immediately.

Glazed Lamb Meatballs + Tuna Cakes

Cooking period: 15 mins. Serving portions: 4

Glazed Lamb Meatballs: Per Serving: Calories 413, Carbs 39.5g, Fat 11.9 g, Protein 36.2g

Tuna Cakes: Per Serving: Calories: 200, Carbs 2.9g, Fat 10.1g, Protein 23.4g

For the Glazed Lamb Meatballs:	**For the Tuna Cakes:**
For the Meatballs: <ul><li>Lean ground lamb – 1 lb.</li><li>Quick-cooking oats – 5¼ tbsp.</li><li>Ritz crackers – ¼ C. crushed</li><li>Canned evaporated milk – 2½ oz.</li><li>Large-sized egg – 1, whisked lightly</li><li>Maple syrup – ½ tsp.</li><li>Dried onion – ½ tbsp. finely cut up</li><li>Salt and powdered black pepper, as desired</li></ul> **For the Sauce:** <ul><li>Orange marmalade – 3 tbsp.</li><li>Maple syrup – 3 tbsp.</li><li>White sugar – 3 tbsp.</li><li>Cornstarch – 1 tbsp.</li><li>Soy sauce – 1 tbsp.</li><li>Sriracha – 1 tbsp.</li><li>Worcestershire sauce – ½ tbsp.</li></ul>	<ul><li>Tuna – – 2 (6-oz.) cans, liquid removed</li><li>Mayonnaise – 1½ tbsp.</li><li>Almond flour – 1½ tbsp.</li><li>Lemon juice – 1 tbsp.</li><li>Dried dill – 1 tsp.</li><li>Garlic powder – 1 tsp.</li><li>Onion powder – ½ tsp.</li><li>Salt – 1 pinch and powdered black pepper</li></ul>

Method of Cooking:

1. For the meatballs, put ground lamb and remnant ingredients into a large-sized basin and stir to incorporate thoroughly.
2. Make 1½-inch balls from the mixture.
3. To turn on the 2-Basket Air Fryer, press "Power".
4. Then press "Start/Pause" to start cooking.
5. Spray the basket of "Zone 1".
6. Press "Zone 1" and choose "Air Fry".
7. Press "Temp" to adjust at 380ºF and then press "Time" for 5 minutes to preheat.
8. After preheating, lay the meatballs in the "Zone 1" basket.
9. Slide the basket into the Air Fryer and press "Time" to adjust for 15 minutes.

10. Change the side of the meatballs once halfway through.
11. Meanwhile, for the sauce, put marmalade and remnant ingredients into a small-sized saucepan on a burner at around medium heat.
12. Cook until thickened, stirring all the time.
13. Meanwhile, for the tuna cakes, put tuna, mayonnaise, flour, lemon juice, dill, and spices into a large basin and mix to incorporate.
14. Shape the mixture into 4 patties.
15. Spray the basket of "Zone 2".
16. Press "Zone 2" and choose "Air Fry".
17. Press "Temp" to adjust at 400°F and then press "Time" for 5 minutes to preheat.
18. After preheating, lay the tuna cakes in the "Zone 2" basket.
19. Slide the basket into the Air Fryer and press "Time" to adjust for 14 minutes.
20. After 10 minutes of cooking, change the side of the tuna cakes.
21. After cooking time is finished, press "Start/Pause" to stop cooking.
22. Put the meatballs and tuna cakes onto serving plates.
23. Enjoy the meatballs with the topping of sauce.
24. Enjoy tuna cakes moderately hot.

Rice & Beans Stuffed Bell Peppers + Herbed Scallops

Cooking period: 15 mins. | Serving portions: 2

Rice & Beans Stuffed Bell Peppers: Per Serving: Calories 292, Carbs 35.5g, Fat 9.2g, Protein 19.7g

Herbed Sea Scallops: Per Serving: Calories 203, Carbs 4.5g, Fat 7.1g, Protein 28.7g

For the Rice & Beans Stuffed Bell Peppers:	For the Herbed Sea Scallops:
<ul><li>Small-sized bell pepper – ¼, seeds removed and cut up</li><li>Canned diced tomatoes with juice – 6 oz.</li><li>Canned red kidney beans – 5 oz. liquid removed</li><li>Cooked rice – ½ C.</li><li>Italian seasoning – ½ tsp.</li><li>Large-sized bell peppers – 2, tops and seeds removed</li><li>Mozzarella cheese – 3 tbsp. shredded</li><li>Parmesan cheese – 1 tbsp. grated</li></ul>	<ul><li>Sea scallops – ¾ lb. cleaned and pat dry</li><li>Unsalted butter – 1 tbsp. liquefied</li><li>Fresh thyme – ¼ tbsp. finely cut up</li><li>Fresh rosemary – ¼ tbsp. finely cut up</li><li>Salt and powdered black pepper, as desired</li></ul>

Method of Cooking:

1. For the stuffed bell peppers, put cut-up bell peppers, tomatoes with juice, beans, rice, and Italian seasoning into a basin and stir to incorporate.
2. Stuff each bell pepper with rice mixture.
3. Spray the basket of "Zone 1". To turn on the 2-Basket Air Fryer, press "Power".
4. Then press "Start/Pause" to start cooking. Press "Zone 1" and choose "Air Fry".
5. Press "Temp" to adjust at 360°F and then press "Time" for 5 minutes to preheat.
6. After preheating, lay the bell peppers in the "Zone 1" basket.
7. Slide the basket into the Air Fryer and press "Time" to adjust for 15 minutes.
8. Meanwhile, put mozzarella and Parmesan cheese into a basin and stir to incorporate.
9. After 12 minutes of cooking, top each bell pepper with the cheese mixture.
10. Meanwhile, for the scallops, put scallops, butter, herbs, salt, and pepper into a large basin and toss to incorporate thoroughly.
11. For the scallops, spray the basket of "Zone 1".
12. Press "Zone 2" and choose "Air Fry".
13. Press "Temp" to adjust at 390°F and then press "Time" for 5 minutes to preheat.
14. After preheating, lay the scallops in the "Zone 2" basket.
15. Slide the basket into the Air Fryer and press "Time" to adjust for 4 minutes.
16. After cooking time is finished, press "Start/Pause" to stop cooking.
17. Take out the bell peppers and scallops from the Air Fryer. Enjoy hot.

Appetizer & Side Dish Recipes

Kale Chips + Parmesan Brussels Sprouts

Cooking period: 5 mins. | Serving portions: 4

Kale Chips: Per Serving: Calories 143, Carbs 23.8g, Fat 3.5g, Protein 6.9g

Parmesan Brussels Sprout: Per Serving: Calories 127, Carbs 15.4g, Fat 5.6g, Protein 6.7g

For the Kale Chips:	For the Parmesan Brussels Sprouts:
• Fresh kale head – 1, stems and ribs removed and cut into 1½-inch pieces • Olive oil – 1 tbsp. • Soy sauce – 1 tsp. • Cayenne pepper powder – 1/8 tsp. • Pinch of powdered black pepper	• Brussels sprouts – 1 lb. trimmed and halved • Balsamic vinegar – 1 tbsp. • Olive oil – 1 tbsp. • Salt and powdered black pepper, as desired • Whole-wheat breadcrumbs – ¼ C. • Parmesan cheese – ¼ C. shredded

Method of Cooking:

1. For the kale chips, put kale pieces and remnant ingredients into a large basin and stir to incorporate thoroughly.
2. To turn on the 2-Basket Air Fryer, press "Power".
3. Then press "Start/Pause" to start cooking.
4. Spray the basket of "Zone 1".
5. Press "Zone 1" and choose "Air Fry".
6. Press "Temp" to adjust at 390°F and then press "Time" for 5 minutes to preheat.
7. After preheating, lay out the kale pieces in the "Zone 1" basket.
8. While cooking, toss the kale pieces once halfway through.
9. Meanwhile, spray the basket of "Zone 2" for the Brussels sprouts.
10. Press "Zone 2" and choose "Air Fry".
11. Press "Temp" to adjust at 400°F and then press "Time" for 5 minutes to preheat.
12. Put the Brussels sprout, vinegar, oil, salt, and pepper into a basin and toss to incorporate thoroughly.
13. After preheating, lay out the Brussels sprouts into the "Zone 2" basket.
14. Slide the basket into the Air Fryer and press "Time" to adjust for 10 minutes.
15. After 5 minutes of cooking, change the side of Brussels sprouts and sprinkle with breadcrumbs, followed by the cheese.
16. After cooking time is finished, press "Start/Pause" to stop cooking.   Take out the kale chips and Brussels sprouts from the Air Fryer.
17. Enjoy the Brussels sprout hot. Let the kale chips cool before enjoying them.

Potato Fries + Glazed Mushrooms

Cooking period: 16 mins. | Serving portions: 2

Potato Fries: Per Serving: Calories 138, Carbs 17.8g, Fat 7.1g, Protein 1.9g

Glazed Mushrooms: Per Serving: Calories 105, Carbs 20.1g, Fat 0.2g, Protein 4g

For the Potato Fries:	For the Glazed Mushrooms:
• Potatoes – ½ lb. peel removed and cut into ½-inch thick sticks lengthwise • Olive oil – 1 tbsp. • Salt and powdered black pepper, as desired	• Soy sauce – 2 tbsp. • Maple syrup – 2 tbsp. • Rice vinegar – 2 tbsp. • Garlic clove – 1, finely cut up • Chinese five-spice powder – 1 tsp. • Powdered ginger – ½ tsp. • Fresh cremini mushrooms – 8 oz. halved

Method of Cooking:

1. For the fries: To turn on the 2-Basket Air Fryer, press "Power".
2. Then press "Start/Pause" to start cooking.
3. Lightly spray the basket of "Zone 1".
4. Press "Zone 1" and choose "Air Fry".
5. Press "Temp" to adjust to 400°F and then press "Time" for 5 minutes to preheat.
6. Put potato sticks and remnant ingredients into a large-sized basin and toss to incorporate thoroughly.
7. After preheating, lay the potato sticks in the "Zone 1" basket.
8. Slide the basket into the Air Fryer and press "Time" to adjust for 16 minutes.
9. While cooking, change the side of the potato sticks once halfway through.
10. Meanwhile, press "Zone 2" for the mushrooms and choose "Air Fry".
11. Press "Temp" to adjust at 350°F and then press "Time" for 5 minutes to preheat.
12. Put soy sauce, maple syrup, vinegar, garlic, five-spice powder, and ginger into a basin and stir to incorporate thoroughly.
13. Place the mushrooms into a greased baking pan.
14. After preheating, lay the baking pan into the "Zone 2" basket.
15. Slide the basket into the Air Fryer and press "Time" to adjust for 15 minutes.
16. After cooking time is finished, press "Start/Pause" to stop cooking.
17. Take off the fries and mushrooms from the Air Fryer.
18. Enjoy hot.

Jalapeño Poppers + Spiced Zucchini

Cooking period: 15 mins. | Serving portions: 6

Jalapeño Poppers: Per Serving: Calories 171, Carbs 3.7g, Fat 15.7g, Protein 4.9g

Spiced Zucchini: Per Serving: Calories 54, Carbs 4g, Fat 15.6g, Protein 1.5g

For the Jalapeño Poppers:	For Spiced Zucchini:
<ul><li>Large-sized jalapeño peppers – 12</li><li>Cream cheese – 8 oz. softened</li><li>Scallion – ¼ C. cut up</li><li>Fresh cilantro – ¼ C. cut up</li><li>Onion powder – ¼ tsp.</li><li>Garlic powder – ¼ tsp.</li><li>Salt, as desired</li><li>Sharp cheddar cheese – 1/3 C. grated</li></ul>	<ul><li>Zucchini – 1½ lb. slivered</li><li>Unsalted butter – 2 tbsp. liquefied</li><li>Dried rosemary – ½ tsp. crushed</li><li>Powdered cumin – ½ tsp.</li><li>Powdered coriander – ½ tsp.</li><li>Cayenne pepper powder – ½ tsp.</li><li>Salt and powdered black pepper, as desired</li></ul>

Method of Cooking:

1. For the poppers: carefully cut off one-third of each pepper lengthwise and then scoop out the seeds and membranes.
2. Put cream cheese, scallion, cilantro, spices, and salt into a basin and stir to incorporate.
3. Stuff each pepper with the cream cheese mixture and top with cheese.
4. To turn on the 2-Basket Air Fryer, press "Power".
5. Then press "Start/Pause" to start cooking.
6. Spray the basket of "Zone 1".
7. Press "Zone 1" and choose "Air Fry".
8. Press "Temp" to adjust at 400°F and then press "Time" for 5 minutes to preheat.
9. After preheating, lay out the jalapeño peppers into the "Zone 1" basket.
10. Slide the basket into the Air Fryer and press "Time" to adjust for 13 minutes.
11. Meanwhile, spray the basket of "Zone 2" for the zucchini.
12. Press "Zone 2" and choose "Air Fry".
13. Press "Temp" to adjust at 390°F and then press "Time" for 5 minutes to preheat.
14. Put zucchini and remnant ingredients into a large basin and stir to incorporate thoroughly.
15. After preheating, lay out the zucchini slices in the "Zone 2" basket.
16. Slide the basket into the Air Fryer and press "Time" to adjust for 15 minutes.
17. After cooking time is finished, press "Start/Pause" to stop cooking.
18. Take out the poppers and zucchini slices from the Air Fryer.
19. Enjoy the zucchini hot.
20. Enjoy the poppers moderately hot.

Spicy Chickpeas + Herbed Carrots

Cooking period: 10 mins.	Serving portions: 2

Spicy Chickpeas: Per Serving: Calories 159, Carbs 24.4g, Fat 4.8g, Protein 5.4g

Herbed Carrots: Per Serving: Calories 93, Carbs 12.5g, Fat 4.8g, Protein 1.3g

For the Spicy Chickpeas:	For the Herbed Carrots:
• Chickpeas – ½ (15-oz.) can, liquid removed • Olive oil – ½ tbsp. • Powdered cumin – ¼ tsp. • Cayenne pepper powder – ¼ tsp. • Paprika – ¼ tsp. • Salt, as desired	• Heirloom carrots – ½ lb. peel removed • Fresh thyme – 1 tbsp. finely cut up • Fresh tarragon leaves – 1 tbsp. finely cut up • Olive oil – 2 tsp. • Salt and powdered black pepper, as desired

Method of Cooking:

1. For the chickpeas: To turn on the 2-Basket Air Fryer, press "Power".
2. Then press "Start/Pause" to start cooking.
3. Lightly spray the basket of "Zone 1".
4. Press "Zone 1" and choose "Air Fry".
5. Press "Temp" to adjust to 390°F and then press "Time" for 5 minutes to preheat.
6. Put chickpeas and remnant ingredients into a basin and toss to incorporate thoroughly.
7. After preheating, place the chickpeas into the "Zone 1" basket.
8. Slide the basket into the Air Fryer and press "Time" to adjust for 10 minutes.
9. Meanwhile, spray the basket of "Zone 2" for the carrots.
10. Press "Zone 2" and choose "Bake".
11. Press "Temp" to adjust to 400°F and then press "Time" for 5 minutes to preheat.
12. Put carrots and remnant ingredients into a basin and toss to incorporate thoroughly.
13. After preheating, place the carrots in the "Zone 2" basket.
14. Slide the basket into the Air Fryer and press "Time" to adjust for 10 minutes.
15. After cooking time is finished, press "Start/Pause" to stop cooking.
16. Take out the chickpeas and carrots from the Air Fryer.
17. Enjoy the carrots hot.
18. Enjoy the chickpeas moderately hot.

Roasted Peanuts + Jacket Potatoes

Cooking period: 15 mins. | Serving portions: 6

Roasted Peanuts: Per Serving: Calories 207, Carbs 5.9g, Fat 18g, Protein 9.4g

Jacket Potatoes: Per Serving: Calories 279, Carbs 34.8g, Fat 12.5g, Protein 8.3g

For the Roasted Peanuts:	For the Jacket Potatoes:
• Raw peanuts – 1½ C. • Anti-sticking baking spray	• Potatoes – 6 • Mozzarella cheese – 4 tbsp. shredded • Sour cream – ½ C. • Unsalted butter – 3 tbsp. softened • Fresh chives – 1 tbsp. finely cut up • Salt and powdered black pepper, as desired

Method of Cooking:

1. To turn on the 2-Basket Air Fryer for the peanuts, press "Power".
2. Then press "Start/Pause" to start cooking.
3. Press "Zone 1" and choose "Air Fry".
4. Press "Temp" to adjust to 320°F and then press "Time" for 5 minutes to preheat.
5. After preheating, place the peanuts into the "Zone 1" basket.
6. Slide the basket into the Air Fryer and press "Time" to adjust for 14 minutes.
7. After 9 minutes of cooking, spray the peanuts with baking spray.
8. While cooking, toss the peanuts twice.
9. Meanwhile, spray the basket of "Zone 2" for the potatoes.
10. Press "Zone 2" and choose "Air Fry".
11. Press "Temp" to adjust to 355°F and then press "Time" for 5 minutes to preheat.
12. With a fork, prick the potatoes.
13. After preheating, place the potatoes into the "Zone 2" basket.
14. Slide the basket into the Air Fryer and press "Time" to adjust for 15 minutes.
15. Meanwhile, put remnant ingredients into a basin and stir to incorporate thoroughly.
16. After cooking time is finished, press "Start/Pause" to stop cooking.
17. Take out the peanuts and potatoes from the Air Fryer.
18. Place the potatoes onto a platter.
19. Open potatoes from the centre and stuff them with cheese mixture.
20. Enjoy the potatoes immediately.

Fish & Seafood Recipes

Miso Glazed Salmon + Spiced Trout

Cooking period: 8 mins. | Serving portions: 4

Glazed Salmon: Per Serving: Calories 335, Carbs 18.3g, Fat 16.6g, Protein 29.8g

Spiced Trout: Per Serving: Calories 230, Carbs 1.2g, Fat 10.7g, Protein 33.3g

For the Miso Glazed Salmon:	For the Spiced Trout:
<ul><li>Sake – 1/3 C.</li><li>White sugar – ¼ C.</li><li>Red miso – ¼ C.</li><li>Soy sauce – 1 tbsp.</li><li>Vegetable oil – 2 tbsp.</li><li>Skinless salmon fillets – 4 (5-oz.) (1-inch thick)</li></ul>	<ul><li>Trout fillets – 1½ lb.</li><li>Red chili powder – 1 tsp.</li><li>Salt and powdered black pepper, as desired</li><li>Lime – 1, cut into slices</li><li>Fresh dill – 1 tbsp. cut up</li></ul>

Method of Cooking:

1. For the salmon, put the sake, sugar, miso, soy sauce, and oil into a basin and whisk to incorporate thoroughly.
2. Rub the salmon fillets with the mixture.
3. Put the salmon into a plastic zip-lock bag.
4. Seal the bag and place it in your refrigerator to marinate for around 30 minutes.
5. Remove the salmon fillets from the bag and shake off the excess marinade.
6. To turn on the 2-Basket Air Fryer, press "Power".
7. Then press "Start/Pause" to start cooking.
8. Spray the basket of "Zone 1".
9. Press "Zone 1" and choose "Air Broil".
10. Press "Time" to adjust for 5 minutes to preheat.
11. After preheating, lay the salmon fillets in the "Zone 1" basket.
12. Slide the basket into the Air Fryer and press "Time" to adjust for 5 minutes.
13. Meanwhile, for the trout, rub the trout fillets with chili powder, salt, and pepper.
14. Spray the basket of "Zone 2".
15. Press "Zone 2" and choose "Air Fry".
16. Press "Temp" to adjust at 375°F and then press "Time" for 5 minutes to preheat.
17. After preheating, lay out the trout fillets into the "Zone 2" basket and top each with lime slices.
18. Slide the basket into the Air Fryer and press "Time" to adjust for 8 minutes.
19. After cooking time is finished, press "Start/Pause" to stop cooking.
20. Take out the salmon and trout fillets from Air Fryer" and enjoy hot.

Lemony Salmon + Tangy Sea Bass

Cooking period: 12 mins. | Serving portions: 2

Lemony Salmon: Per Serving: Calories 297, Carbs 0.8g, Fat 15.8g, Protein 38.7g

Tangy Sea Bass: Per Serving: Calories 241, Carbs 0.9 g, Fat 10.7g, Protein 33.7g

For the Lemony Salmon:	For the Tangy Sea Bass:
<ul><li>Lemon juice – 1 tbsp.</li><li>Olive oil – ½ tbsp.</li><li>Salt and powdered black pepper, as desired</li><li>Garlic clove – 1, finely cut up</li><li>Fresh thyme leaves – ½ tsp., cut up</li><li>Salmon fillets – 2 (7-oz.)</li></ul>	<ul><li>Sea bass fillets – 2 (5 oz.)</li><li>Garlic clove – 1, finely cut up</li><li>Fresh dill – 1 tsp., finely cut up</li><li>Olive oil – 1 tbsp.</li><li>Balsamic vinegar – 1 tbsp.</li><li>Salt and powdered black pepper, as desired</li></ul>

Method of Cooking:

1. For the salmon: put lemon juice and remnant ingredients except for the salmon into a basin and stir to incorporate thoroughly.
2. Put in salmon fillets and coat with the mixture.
3. Coat the fillets with flour mixture, dip them into the egg mixture, and coat with the cornflake mixture.
4. To turn on the 2-Basket Air Fryer, press "Power".
5. Then press "Start/Pause" to start cooking.
6. Spray the basket of "Zone 1".
7. Press "Zone 1" and choose "Air Fry".
8. Press "Temp" to adjust to 400°F and then press "Time" for 5 minutes to preheat.
9. After preheating, lay the salmon fillets in the "Zone 1" basket, skin-side down.
10. Slide the basket into the Air Fryer and press "Time" to adjust for 10 minutes.
11. Change the side of the fillets once halfway through.
12. Meanwhile, for the sea bass:
13. Put fish fillets and remnant ingredients into a large-sized resealable bag.
14. Seal the bag and shake to mix thoroughly.
15. Place into your refrigerator to marinate for at least 30 minutes.
16. Remove the fish fillets from the bag and shake off the excess marinade.
17. Spray the basket of "Zone 2".
18. Press "Zone 2" and choose "Bake".
19. Press "Temp" to adjust to 450°F and then press "Time" for 5 minutes to preheat.
20. After preheating, lay the fish fillets in the "Zone 2" basket.
21. Slide the basket into the Air Fryer and press "Time" to adjust for 12 minutes.
22. After cooking time is finished, press "Start/Pause" to stop cooking.
23. Take out the fish fillets from the Air Fryer and enjoy hot.

Seasoned Catfish + Buttered Salmon

Cooking period: 23 mins. | Serving portions: 4

Seasoned Catfish: Per Serving: Calories 183, Carbs 0.1g, Fat 12.1g, Protein 17.7g

Buttered Salmon: Per Serving: Calories 276, Carbs 0g, Fat 16.3g, Protein 33.1g

For the Seasoned Catfish:	For the Buttered Salmon:
<ul><li>Catfish fillets – 4 (4 oz.)</li><li>Louisiana fish fry seasoning – ¼ C.</li><li>Olive oil – 1 tbsp.</li><li>Fresh parsley – 1 tbsp., cut up</li></ul>	<ul><li>Salmon fillets – 4 (6-oz.)</li><li>Salt and powdered black pepper, as desired</li><li>Unsalted butter – 2 tbsp. liquefied</li></ul>

Method of Cooking:

1. For the catfish: rub the fish fillets with seasoning and then coat them with oil.
2. To turn on the 2-Basket Air Fryer, press "Power".
3. Then press "Start/Pause" to start cooking.
4. Spray the basket of "Zone 1".
5. Press "Zone 1" and choose "Air Fry".
6. Press "Temp" to adjust to 400°F and then press "Time" to adjust for 5 minutes to preheat.
7. After preheating, lay the fish fillets in the "Zone 1" basket.
8. Slide the basket into the Air Fryer and press "Time" to adjust for 23 minutes.
9. After 10 minutes, change the side of the fish fillets.
10. Meanwhile, for the salmon, rub the salmon fillets with salt and pepper and then coat them with butter.
11. Spray the basket of "Zone 2".
12. Press "Zone 2" and choose "Air Broil".
13. Press "Time" to adjust for 5 minutes to preheat.
14. After preheating, lay the salmon fillets in the "Zone 2" basket.
15. Slide the basket into the Air Fryer and press "Time" to adjust for 12 minutes.
16. After cooking time is finished, press "Start/Pause" to stop cooking.
17. Take out the fish fillets from the Air Fryer and enjoy hot.

Cod & Veggie Parcel + Cajun Salmon

Cooking period: 15 mins. | Serving portions: 2

Cod & Veggie Parcel: Per Serving: Calories 306, Carbs 6.8g, Fat 20g, Protein 26.3g

Cajun Salmon: Per Serving: Calories 225, Carbs 0g, Fat 10.5g, Protein 22.1g

For the Cod & Veggie Parcel:	For the Cajun Salmon:
<ul><li>Unsalted butter – 2 tbsp. liquefied</li><li>Lemon juice – 1 tbsp.</li><li>Dried tarragon – ½ tsp.</li><li>Salt and powdered black pepper, as desired</li><li>Bell peppers – ½ C. seeds removed and slivered thinly</li><li>Carrots – ½ C. peel removed and julienned</li><li>Fennel bulbs – ½ C. julienned</li><li>Frozen cod fillets – 2 (5 oz.), thawed</li><li>Olive oil – 1 tbsp.</li></ul>	<ul><li>Salmon steaks – 2 (6 oz.)</li><li>Cajun seasoning – 2 tbsp.</li></ul>

Method of Cooking:

1. For the cod parcel, put the butter, lemon juice, tarragon, salt, and pepper into a large basin and mix to incorporate thoroughly. Add bell pepper, carrot, and fennel bulb and coat with the mixture.
2. Lay out 2 Large-sized bakery paper squares onto a smooth counter.
3. Coat the cod fillets with oil and sprinkle with salt and pepper.
4. Lay out 1 cod fillet onto each parchment square and top each with the vegetables.
5. Top with any remnant sauce from the bowl.
6. Fold the bakery paper and crimp the sides to secure the fish and vegetables.
7. To turn on the 2-Basket Air Fryer, press "Power".
8. Then press "Start/Pause" to start cooking. Spray the basket of "Zone 1". Press "Zone 1" and choose "Air Fry".
9. Press "Temp" to adjust to 350°F and then press "Time" to adjust for 5 minutes to preheat.
10. After preheating, lay out the fish parcels in the "Zone 1" basket.
11. Slide the basket into the Air Fryer and press "Time" to adjust for 15 minutes.
12. Meanwhile, rub the salmon steaks with the Cajun seasoning. Put them aside for around 10 minutes.
13. Spray the basket of "Zone 2". Press "Zone 2" and choose "Air Fry".
14. Press "Temp" to adjust to 390°F and then press "Time" for 5 minutes to preheat.
15. After preheating, lay out the salmon steaks in the "Zone 2" basket.
16. Slide the basket into the Air Fryer and press "Time" to adjust for 8 minutes.
17. After 4 minutes of cooking, change the side of the salmon steaks.
18. After cooking time is finished, press "Start/Pause" to stop cooking.
19. Take off the cod parcels and salmon steaks from Air Fryer.
20. Enjoy salmon steaks hot.
21. Put the parcels onto serving plates. Carefully open each parcel and enjoy moderately hot.

Crusted Salmon + Shrimp Scampi

Cooking period: 15 mins. | Serving portions: 3 |

Crusted Salmon: Per Serving: Calories 471, Carbs 5.7g, Fat 33.99g, Protein 36.6g

Shrimp Scampi: Per Serving: Calories 245, Carbs 3.1g, Fat 15.7g, Protein 26.4g

For the Crusted Salmon:	For the Shrimp Scampi:
<ul><li>Skinless salmon fillets – 3 (6 oz.)</li><li>Salt and powdered black pepper, as desired</li><li>Walnuts – 4 tbsp. finely cut up</li><li>Quick-cooking oats – 4 tbsp. crushed</li><li>Olive oil – 2 tbsp.</li></ul>	<ul><li>Salted butter – 4 tbsp.</li><li>Lemon juice – 1 tbsp.</li><li>Garlic – 1 tbsp. finely cut up</li><li>Red pepper flakes – 2 tsp. crushed</li><li>Shrimp – 1 lb. peeled and deveined</li><li>Fresh basil – 2 tbsp. cut up</li><li>Fresh chives – 1 tbsp., cut up</li><li>Chicken broth – 2 tbsp.</li></ul>

Method of Cooking:

1. For the salmon: rub the salmon fillets with salt and black pepper evenly.
2. Put walnuts, oats, and oil into a basin and stir to incorporate.
3. Place the oat mixture over the salmon fillets and gently press down.
4. To turn on the 2-Basket Air Fryer, press "Power".
5. Then press "Start/Pause" to start cooking.
6. Spray the basket of "Zone 1".
7. Press "Zone 1" and choose "Bake".
8. Press "Temp" to adjust to 400⁰F and then press "Time" for 5 minutes to preheat.
9. After preheating, lay the salmon fillets in the "Zone 1" basket.
10. Slide the basket into the Air Fryer and press "Time" to adjust for 15 minutes.
11. Meanwhile, Press "Zone 2" for the shrimp and choose "Air Fry".
12. Lay a 7-inch round baking pan in the "Zone 2" basket.
13. Press "Temp" to adjust to 325⁰F and then press "Time" for 5 minutes to preheat.
14. After preheating, take out the hot pan from the Air Fryer.
15. Put butter, lemon juice, garlic, and red pepper flakes into the hot pan and stir to incorporate thoroughly.
16. Lay out the baking pan into the "Zone 2" basket.
17. Slide the basket into the Air Fryer and press "Time" to adjust for 7 minutes.
18. After 2 minutes of cooking, stir in the shrimp, basil, chives and broth.
19. After cooking time is finished, press "Start/Pause" to stop cooking.
20. Take out the salmon fillets and baking pan from the Air Fryer.
21. Put the pan of shrimp scampi aside for around 2 minutes.
22. Enjoy hot.

Poultry & Seafood Recipes

Simple Whole Chicken + Breaded Chicken Breasts

Cooking period: 40 mins. Serving portions: 3

Simple Whole chicken: Per Serving: Calories 431, Carbs 0g, Fat 16.8g, Protein 65.6g

Breaded Chicken Breasts: Per Serving: Calories 371, Carbs 13.1g, Fat 18g, Protein 38g

For the Simple Whole Chicken	For the Breaded Chicken Breasts:
<ul><li>Whole chicken – 1 (1½-lb.) , giblets removed</li><li>Dried rosemary – 2 tsp. crushed</li><li>Salt and powdered black pepper, as desired</li></ul>	<ul><li>Breadcrumbs – ½ C.</li><li>Parmesan cheese – ¼ C. grated</li><li>Fresh parsley – 2 tbsp. finely cut up</li><li>Salt and powdered black pepper, as desired</li><li>Boneless chicken breasts – 3 (4 oz.)</li><li>Olive oil – 2 tbsp.</li><li>Olive oil baking spray</li></ul>

Method of Cooking:

1. Rub the chicken with rosemary, salt and pepper.
2. To turn on the 2-Basket Air Fryer, press "Power".
3. Then press "Start/Pause" to start cooking.
4. Spray the basket of "Zone 1". Press "Zone 1" and choose "Air Fry".
5. Press "Temp" to adjust to 390°F and then press "Time" to adjust for 5 minutes to preheat.
6. After preheating, lay the chicken in the "Zone 1" basket, breast-side down.
7. Slide the basket into the Air Fryer and press "Time" to adjust for 40 minutes.
8. Meanwhile, for the chicken breasts, put the breadcrumbs, Parmesan cheese, parsley, salt, and pepper into a shallow dish and stir to incorporate thoroughly.
9. Rub the chicken breasts with oil and coat with the breadcrumbs mixture.
10. Spray the basket of "Zone 2". Press "Zone 2" and choose "Air Fry".
11. Press "Temp" to adjust to 350°F and then press "Time" for 5 minutes to preheat.
12. After preheating, lay the chicken breasts in the "Zone 2" basket.
13. Slide the basket into the Air Fryer and press "Time" to adjust for 12 minutes.
14. Change the side of chicken breasts once halfway through.
15. After cooking time is finished, press "Start/Pause" to stop cooking.
16. Take out the chicken and chicken breasts from Air Fryer.
17. Enjoy the chicken breasts hot.
18. Place the chicken onto a platter for 5-10 minutes before carving.
19. Cut the chicken into serving portions and enjoy.

Spiced Whole Chicken + Herbed Turkey Breast

Cooking period: 1 hr. | Serving portions: 8

Spiced Whole Chicken: Per Serving: Calories 435, Carbs 1g, Fat 213.26.6g, Protein 74.2g

Herbed Turkey Breast: Per Serving: Calories 214, Carbs 8.1g, Fat 6.6g, Protein 29.4g

For the Spiced Whole Chicken:	For the Herbed Turkey Breast:
<ul><li>Dried thyme – 1 tsp. crushed</li><li>Dried rosemary – 1 tsp. crushed</li><li>Dried oregano – 1 tsp. crushed</li><li>Paprika – 2 tsp.</li><li>Powdered cumin – 1 tsp.</li><li>Garlic powder – ½ tsp.</li><li>Onion powder – ½ tsp.</li><li>Salt and powdered black pepper, as desired</li><li>Whole chicken – 1 (4½-lb.), giblets removed</li><li>Olive oil – 3 tbsp. divided</li></ul>	<ul><li>Olive oil – 2 tbsp.</li><li>Lemon juice – 2 tbsp.</li><li>Garlic – 1 tbsp. finely cut up</li><li>Ground mustard – 2 tsp.</li><li>Salt and powdered black pepper, as desired</li><li>Dried sage – 1 tsp.</li><li>Dried thyme – 1 tsp.</li><li>Dried rosemary – 1 tsp.</li><li>Turkey breast – 1 (3-lb.)</li></ul>

Method of Cooking:

1. For the chicken, put herbs, spices, salt, and pepper into a basin and stir to incorporate.
2. Coat the chicken with 2 tbsp. Rub oil inside, outside, and underneath the skin with half of the herb mixture.
3. To turn on the 2-Basket Air Fryer, press "Power".
4. Then press "Start/Pause" to start cooking. Spray the basket of "Zone 1". Press "Zone 1" and choose "Air Fry".
5. Press "Temp" to adjust to 360°F and then press "Time" for 5 minutes to preheat.
6. After preheating, lay the chicken in the "Zone 1" basket.
7. Slide the basket into the Air Fryer and press "Time" to adjust for 60 minutes, breast-side down.
8. After 30 minutes of cooking, change the side of the chicken once halfway through.
9. Coat the chicken with remnant oil and then rub it with the remnant herb mixture.
10. Meanwhile, for the turkey breast, put oil and remnant ingredients except the turkey breast into a small basin and mix to incorporate thoroughly. Rub the oil mixture outside the turkey breast and on any loose skin.
11. Spray the basket of "Zone 2". Press "Zone 2" and choose "Air Fry".
12. Press "Temp" to adjust to 360°F and then press "Time" for 5 minutes to preheat.
13. After preheating, lay the turkey breast into the "Zone 2" basket, skin side up.
14. Slide the basket into the Air Fryer and press "Time" to adjust for 60 minutes.
15. After cooking time is finished, press "Start/Pause" to stop cooking.
16. Take out the chicken and turkey breast from the Air Fryer.
17. Place the chicken and turkey breast onto a platter for 5-10 minutes.
18. Cut the chicken and turkey breast into serving portions and enjoy.

Buttered Turkey Wings + BBQ Chicken Breasts

Cooking period: 26 mins. | Serving portions: 4

Buttered Turkey Wings: Per Serving: Calories 546, Carbs 0g, Fat 31g, Protein 62.8g

BBQ Chicken Breasts: Per Serving: Calories 585, Carbs 22.7g, Fat 24g, Protein 65.6g

For the Buttered Turkey Wings:	For the BBQ Chicken Breasts:
• Turkey wings – 2 lb. • Salt and powdered black pepper, as desired • Unsalted butter – 3 tbsp. liquefied	• Frozen boneless chicken breasts – 4 (8 oz.) • Olive oil – 2 tbsp. divided • Salt and powdered black pepper, as desired • BBQ sauce – 1 C.

Method of Cooking:

1. For the turkey wings: put the turkey wings, butter, salt, and pepper into a large-sized basin and mix to incorporate thoroughly.
2. To turn on the 2-Basket Air Fryer, press "Power".
3. Then press "Start/Pause" to start cooking.
4. Spray the basket of "Zone 1".
5. Press "Zone 1" and choose "Air Fry".
6. Press "Temp" to adjust to 380°F and then press "Time" for 5 minutes to preheat.
7. After preheating, lay the turkey wings in the "Zone 1" basket.
8. Slide the basket into the Air Fryer and press "Time" to adjust for 26 minutes.
9. After 14 minutes of cooking, change the side of the turkey wings.
10. Meanwhile, for the chicken breasts, brush the chicken breasts with – ½ tbsp. of oil and rub with salt and pepper.
11. Spray the basket of "Zone 2".
12. Press "Zone 2" and choose "Air Broil."
13. Press "Time" to adjust for 5 minutes to preheat.
14. After preheating, lay the chicken breasts in the "Zone 2" basket.
15. Slide the basket into the Air Fryer and press "Time" to adjust for 22 minutes.
16. After first 10 minutes, change the side of the chicken breasts.
17. After 5 minutes more, change the side of the chicken breasts and coat the upper side with BBQ sauce.
18. After 5 minutes more, change the side of the chicken breasts and coat the upper side with BBQ sauce.
19. After cooking time is finished, press "Start/Pause" to stop cooking.
20. Take out the turkey wings and chicken breasts from the Air Fryer and enjoy hot.

Spicy Chicken Thighs + Crispy Chicken Drumsticks

Cooking period: 25 mins. | Serving portions: 4

Spicy Chicken Thighs: Per Serving: Calories 204, Carbs 0.4g, Fat 11.2g, Protein 25.4g

Crispy Chicken drumsticks: Per Serving: Calories 483, Carbs 35.1g, Fat 12.5g, Protein 53.7g

For Spicy Chicken Thighs:	For the Crispy Chicken drumsticks:
<ul><li>Boneless chicken thighs – 4 (4 oz.)</li><li>Cayenne pepper powder – ½ tsp.</li><li>Paprika – ½ tsp.</li><li>Powdered cumin – ½ tsp.</li><li>Salt and powdered black pepper, as desired</li><li>Olive oil – 2 tbsp.</li></ul>	<ul><li>Chicken drumsticks – 4</li><li>Adobo seasoning – 1 tbsp.</li><li>Salt, as desired</li><li>Paprika – ½ tbsp.</li><li>Onion powder – 1 tsp.</li><li>Garlic powder – 1 tsp.</li><li>Powdered black pepper, as desired</li><li>Eggs – 2</li><li>Milk – 2 tbsp.</li><li>All-purpose flour – 1 C.</li><li>Cornstarch – ¼ C.</li></ul>

Method of Cooking:

1. For the chicken thighs, put spices, salt, and pepper into a basin and stir to incorporate.
2. Rub the chicken thighs with the spice mixture and then brush with oil.
3. To turn on the 2-Basket Air Fryer, press "Power".
4. Then press "Start/Pause" to start cooking.
5. Spray the basket of "Zone 1".
6. Press "Zone 1" and choose "Bake".
7. Press "Temp" to adjust to 450⁰F and then press "Time" for 5 minutes to preheat.
8. After preheating, lay the chicken thighs into the "Zone 1" basket.
9. Slide the basket into the Air Fryer and press "Time" to adjust for 20 minutes.
10. Meanwhile, for the chicken drumsticks, rub chicken drumsticks with adobo seasoning and a pinch of salt.
11. Put it aside for around 5 minutes.
12. Put the spices, salt, and pepper into a small basin and stir to incorporate thoroughly.
13. Put the eggs, milk, and 1 tsp. of the spice mixture into a shallow basin and whisk to incorporate thoroughly.
14. Put the flour, cornstarch, and remnant spice mixture into another shallow basin and stir to incorporate.
15. Coat the chicken drumsticks with flour mixture and tap off the excess.
16. Now, dip the chicken drumsticks in the egg mixture.
17. Again, coat the chicken drumsticks with flour mixture.
18. Lay the chicken drumsticks onto a wire rack-lined baking sheet and put it aside for around 15 minutes.
19. Spray the basket of "Zone 2".
20. Press "Zone 2" and choose "Air Fry".

21. Press "Temp" to adjust to 350°F and then press "Time" for 5 minutes to preheat.
22. After preheating, lay the chicken drumsticks in the "Zone 2" basket.
23. Spray the chicken drumsticks with baking spray lightly.
24. Slide the basket into the Air Fryer and press "Time" to adjust for 25 minutes.
25. After cooking time is finished, press "Start/Pause" to stop cooking.
26. Take out the chicken thighs and drumsticks from Air Fryer and enjoy hot.

Herbed Whole Chicken + Glazed Turkey Breast

Cooking period: 1 hr. | Serving portions: 10

Herbed Whole Chicken: Per Serving: Calories 860, Carbs 1.3g, Fat 50g, Protein 71.1g

Glazed Turkey Breast: Per Serving: Calories 252, Carbs 5.4g, Fat 2.3g, Protein 56.4g

For the Herbed Whole Chicken:	For the Glazed Turkey Breast:
<ul><li>Garlic cloves – 3, finely cut up</li><li>Lemon zest – 1 tsp. finely grated</li><li>Dried thyme – 1 tsp. crushed</li><li>Dried oregano – 1 tsp. crushed</li><li>Dried rosemary – 1 tsp. crushed</li><li>Paprika – 1 tsp.</li><li>Salt and powdered black pepper, as desired</li><li>Lemon juice – 2 tbsp.</li><li>Olive oil – 2 tbsp.</li><li>Whole chicken – 1 (5-lb.)</li></ul>	<ul><li>Boneless turkey breast – 1 (5-lb.)</li><li>Salt and powdered black pepper, as desired</li><li>Honey – 3 tbsp.</li><li>Dijon mustard – 2 tbsp.</li><li>Unsalted butter – 1 tbsp. softened</li></ul>

Method of Cooking:

1. For the chicken, put garlic, lemon zest, herbs, and spices into a basin and stir to incorporate.
2. Rub the chicken with herb mixture. Drizzle the chicken with lemon juice and oil.
3. Put it aside at room temperature for around 40-50 minutes.
4. To turn on the 2-Basket Air Fryer, press "Power".
5. Then press "Start/Pause" to start cooking. Spray the basket of "Zone 1". Press "Zone 1" and choose "Air Fry".
6. Press "Temp" to adjust to 360°F and then press "Time" for 5 minutes to preheat.
7. After preheating, lay the chicken in the "Zone 1" basket, breast side down.
8. Slide the basket into the Air Fryer and press "Time" to adjust for 60 minutes.
9. After 50 minutes of cooking, change the side of the chicken.
10. Meanwhile, for the turkey breast, rub the turkey breast with salt and pepper and spray it with baking spray.
11. Spray the basket of "Zone 2". Press "Zone 2" and choose "Air Fry".
12. Press "Temp" to adjust to 350° and then press "Time" to adjust for 5 minutes to preheat.
13. After preheating, lay the turkey breast in the "Zone 2" basket.
14. Slide the basket into the Air Fryer and press "Time" to adjust for 55 minutes.
15. Meanwhile, put maple syrup, mustard, and butter into a basin for the glaze and stir to incorporate.
16. Change the side of turkey breast twice, first after 25 minutes and then after 37 minutes.
17. After 50 minutes of cooking, coat the turkey breast with the glaze.
18. After cooking time is finished, press "Start/Pause" to stop cooking.
19. Take out the chicken and turkey breast from the Air Fryer.
20. Place the chicken and turkey breast onto a platter for 5-10 minutes.
21. Cut the chicken and turkey breast into serving portions and enjoy.

Crusted Chicken Drumsticks + Thyme Turkey Tenderloins

Cooking period: 20 mins. | Serving portions: 4

Crusted Chicken Drumsticks: Per Serving: Calories: 400, Carbs 22.7g, Fat 11.4g, Protein 48.9g

Thyme Turkey Tenderloin: Per Serving: Calories 244, Carbs 0.7g, Fat 9.2g, Protein 39.3g

For the Crusted Chicken Drumsticks:	For the Thyme Turkey Tenderloin:
<ul><li>Oyster sauce – 1 tbsp.</li><li>Light soy sauce – 1 tsp.</li><li>Sesame oil – ½ tsp.</li><li>Chinese five spice powder – 1 tsp.</li><li>Salt and ground white pepper, as desired</li><li>Chicken drumsticks – 4 (6-oz.)</li><li>Corn flour – 1 C.</li></ul>	<ul><li>Dried thyme – 1 tsp. crushed</li><li>Garlic powder – 1 tsp.</li><li>Salt and powdered black pepper, as desired</li><li>Boneless turkey breast tenderloins – 1 (24-oz.) package</li><li>Olive oil – 2 tbsp.</li></ul>

Method of Cooking:

1. Put sauces, oil, five-spice powder, salt, and pepper into a basin and stir to incorporate for the chicken drumsticks. Put in chicken drumsticks and coat with the marinade.
2. Place into your refrigerator for at least 30-40 minutes.
3. Put the corn flour into a shallow dish. Take the chicken drumsticks from the marinade and lightly coat them with corn flour.
4. To turn on the 2-Basket Air Fryer, press "Power". Then press "Start/Pause" to start cooking.
5. Spray the basket of "Zone 1". Press "Zone 1" and choose "Air Fry".
6. Press "Temp" to adjust to 390°F and then press "Time" for 5 minutes to preheat.
7. After preheating, lay the chicken drumsticks in the "Zone 1" basket.
8. Slide the basket into the Air Fryer and press "Time" to adjust for 20 minutes.
9. After cooking time is finished, press "Start/Pause" to stop cooking.
10. Meanwhile, put thyme, garlic powder, salt, and pepper into a small basin for the turkey and stir to incorporate. Rub the turkey tenderloins with thyme mixture.
11. Sizzle the oil into a wok on a burner at around medium heat.
12. Cook the turkey tenderloins for around 10 minutes or until golden brown.
13. Remove from the burner and place the turkey tenderloins onto a plate.
14. Spray the basket of "Zone 2". Press "Zone 2" and choose "Bake".
15. Press "Temp" to adjust to 350°F and then press "Time" for 5 minutes to preheat.
16. After preheating, lay the turkey tenderloins into the "Zone 2" basket.
17. Slide the basket into the Air Fryer and press "Time" to adjust for 10 minutes.
18. After cooking time is finished, press "Start/Pause" to stop cooking.
19. Take out the chicken drumsticks and turkey tenderloins from the Air Fryer.
20. Place the turkey tenderloins onto a chopping board for around 5 minutes before slicing.
21. Enjoy chicken drumsticks hot.
22. Cut the turkey tenderloins into serving portions and enjoy.

Crispy Chicken Thighs + Chicken & Pineapple Kabobs

Cooking period: 20 mins. | Serving portions: 4

Crispy Chicken Thighs: Per Serving: Calories: 771, Carbs 32.1g, Fat 33.1g, Protein 68.7g

Chicken & Pineapple Kabobs: Per Serving: Calories 296, Carbs 13.8g, Fat 17.3g, Protein 21.1g

For the Crispy Chicken Thighs:	For the Chicken & Pineapple Kabobs:
<ul><li>Chicken thighs – 4 (5 oz.)</li><li>Unsalted buttermilk – ½ C.</li><li>All-purpose flour – ½ C.</li><li>Panko breadcrumbs – ½ C.</li><li>Baking powder – ¼ tsp.</li><li>Dried oregano – ¼ tsp.</li><li>Dried thyme – ¼ tsp.</li><li>Celery salt – ¼ tsp.</li><li>Garlic powder – ¼ tsp.</li><li>Powdered ginger – ¼ tsp.</li><li>Cayenne pepper powder – ¼ tsp.</li><li>Paprika – ¼ tsp.</li><li>Salt and powdered black pepper, as desired</li><li>Unsalted butter – 3 tbsp. liquefied</li></ul>	<ul><li>Boneless chicken thigh fillets – 4 (4 oz.) cut into cubes</li><li>Jerk seasoning – 1 tbsp.</li><li>Large-sized bell peppers – 2, seeds removed and cubed</li><li>Salt and powdered black pepper, as desired</li><li>Canned pineapple chunks – 10 oz. liquid removed</li><li>Jerk sauce – 2 tbsp.</li></ul>

Method of Cooking:

1. For the chicken thighs, put the chicken thighs and buttermilk into a resealable plastic bag.
2. Squeeze the air out and seal the bag tightly.
3. Place into your refrigerator for around 2-3 hours.
4. Put flour, breadcrumbs, baking powder, herbs, and spices into a shallow basin; stir to incorporate thoroughly.
5. Remove the chicken thighs from the bag and shake off the excess buttermilk.
6. Coat chicken thighs with the seasoned flour mixture.
7. To turn on the 2-Basket Air Fryer, press "Power".
8. Then press "Start/Pause" to start cooking.
9. Spray the basket of "Zone 1".
10. Press "Zone 1" and choose "Air Fry".
11. Press "Temp" to adjust to 390°F and then press "Time" for 5 minutes to preheat.
12. After preheating, lay the chicken thighs into the "Zone 1" basket.
13. Slide the basket into the Air Fryer and press "Time" to adjust for 20 minutes.
14. After 10 minutes of cooking, change the side of the chicken thighs and coat them with the liquefied butter.
15. Meanwhile, put chicken cubes and jerk seasoning into a basin for the kabobs and stir to incorporate.

16. Cover the bowl of chicken and place it into your refrigerator overnight.
17. Sprinkle the bell peppers with salt and pepper.
18. Thread the chicken, bell pepper, and pineapple onto greased metal skewers.
19. Spray the basket of "Zone 2".
20. Press "Zone 2" and choose "Air Fry".
21. Press "Temp" to adjust to 370°F and then press "Time" for 5 minutes to preheat.
22. After preheating, lay the skewers in the "Zone 2" basket.
23. Slide the basket into the Air Fryer and press "Time" to adjust for 8-9 minutes.
24. Change the side of the skewers and coat them with jerk sauce once halfway through.
25. After cooking time is finished, press "Start/Pause" to stop cooking.
26. Take out the chicken thighs and skewers from Air Fryer and enjoy hot.

Glazed Duck Breast + Oats Crusted Chicken Breasts

Cooking period: 44 mins. | Serving portions: 3

Glazed Duck Breast: Per Serving: Calories 332, Carbs 33.7g, Fat 6.1g, Protein 34g

Oats-Crusted Chicken Breasts: Per Serving: Calories 363, Carbs 21.4g, Fat 9.1g, Protein 48.7g

For the Glazed Duck Breast:	For the Oats-Crusted Chicken Breasts:
• Pomegranate juice – 2 C. • Lemon juice – 2 tbsp. • Brown sugar – 3 tbsp. • Boneless duck breast – 1 lb.	• Chicken breasts – 3 (6 oz.) • Salt and powdered black pepper, as desired • Oats – 1 C. • Mustard powder – 2 tbsp. • Fresh parsley – 1 tbsp. • Medium-sized eggs – 2

Method of Cooking:

1. For the duck breast, put the pomegranate juice, lemon juice, and brown sugar into a medium-sized saucepan on a burner at around medium heat. Cook the mixture until boiling. Immediately turn the heat to low.
2. Cook for around 25 minutes. Remove the glaze pan from the burner and let it cool slightly.
3. Score the fat of the duck breast several times using a sharp knife.
4. Sprinkle the duck breast with salt and pepper.
5. To turn on the 2-Basket Air Fryer, press "Power". Then press "Start/Pause" to start cooking.
6. Spray the basket of "Zone 1". Press "Zone 1" and choose "Air Fry".
7. Press "Temp" to adjust to 400ºF and then press "Time" for 5 minutes to preheat.
8. After preheating, lay the duck breast into the "Zone 1" basket.
9. Slide the basket into the Air Fryer and press "Time" to adjust for 14 minutes.
10. Change the side of the duck breast once halfway through.
11. Meanwhile, for the chicken breasts, put the chicken breasts onto a chopping board and, with a meat mallet, flatten each into even thicknesses. Then, cut each breast in half.
12. Sprinkle the chicken pieces with salt and pepper and put them aside.
13. Put the oats, mustard powder, parsley, salt, and pepper into a mixer and process to form a coarse breadcrumb-like mixture. Place the oat mixture into a shallow dish. Whisk the eggs into another basin.
14. Coat the chicken with the oat mixture and then dip into whisked eggs and coat with the oats mixture again.
15. Spray the basket of "Zone 2". Press "Zone 2" and choose "Air Fry".
16. Press "Temp" to adjust to 350 ºF and then press "Time" for 5 minutes to preheat.
17. After preheating, lay the chicken breasts in the "Zone 2" basket.
18. Slide the basket into the Air Fryer and press "Time" to adjust for 12 minutes.
19. Change the side of the chicken breast once halfway through.
20. After cooking time is finished, press "Start/Pause" to stop cooking.
21. Take out the duck breast and chicken breasts from the Air Fryer.
22. Enjoy the chicken breasts hot. Place the duck breast onto a chopping board for 5-10 minutes.
23. Drizzle with the warm pomegranate juice mixture and enjoy.

Bacon-Wrapped Chicken Breasts +Buttered Duck Legs

Cooking period: 23 mins. | Serving portions: 4

Bacon-Wrapped Chicken Breasts: Per Serving: Calories: 365, Carbs 2.7g, Fat 24.8g, Protein 30.2g

Buttered Duck Legs: Per Serving: Calories 531, Carbs 0g, Fat 25.9 g, Protein 70.2g

For the Bacon-Wrapped Chicken Breasts:	For the Buttered Duck Legs:
• Fresh basil leaves – 6-7 • Fish sauce – 2 tbsp. • Water – 2 tbsp. • Chicken breasts – 2 (8-oz.), cut each in half horizontally • Salt and powdered black pepper, as desired • Bacon strips – 12 • Honey – 1½ tsp.	• Unsalted butter – ¼ C. liquefied • Duck legs – 4 • Salt and powdered black pepper, as desired

Method of Cooking:

1. Put palm sugar into a small-sized heavy-bottomed pan on a burner for the chicken breasts at medium-low heat.
2. Cook for around 2-3 minutes, stirring all the time.
3. Put in basil, fish sauce, and water and stir to incorporate.
4. Take off the burner and put the sugar mixture into a large-sized basin.
5. Sprinkle each chicken breast with salt and pepper.
6. Put chicken breasts into the sugar mixture and coat.
7. Place into your refrigerator to marinate for around 4-6 hours.
8. Wrap each chicken piece with 3 bacon strips.
9. Coat each piece slightly with honey.
10. To turn on the 2-Basket Air Fryer, press "Power". Then press "Start/Pause" to start cooking.
11. Spray the basket of "Zone 1". Press "Zone 1" and choose "Air Fry".
12. Press "Temp" to adjust to 365°F and then press "Time" for 5 minutes to preheat.
13. After preheating, lay the chicken breasts in the "Zone 1" basket.
14. Slide the basket into the Air Fryer and press "Time" to adjust for 20 minutes.
15. After cooking time is finished, press "Start/Pause" to stop cooking.
16. For the duck legs: coat the duck legs with butter and then rub with salt and pepper.
17. Spray the basket of "Zone 2". Press "Zone 2" and choose "Air Fry".
18. Press "Temp" to adjust to 400°F and then press "Time" for 5 minutes to preheat.
19. After preheating, lay the duck legs in the "Zone 2" basket.
20. Slide the basket into the Air Fryer and press "Time" to adjust for 15 minutes.
21. After cooking time is finished, press "Start/Pause" to stop cooking.
22. Take out the chicken breasts and duck legs from Air Fryer and enjoy hot.

Turkey Meatloaf + Sausage-Stuffed Chicken Breasts

Cooking period: 15 mins. Serving portions: 4

Turkey Meatloaf: Per Serving: Calories: 435, Carbs 18.1g, Fat 23.1g, Protein 42.2g

Sausage-Stuffed Chicken Breasts: Per Serving: Calories: 345, Carbs 0g, Fat 21.1g, Protein 37g

For the Turkey Meatloaf:	For the Sausage-Stuffed Chicken Breasts:
<ul><li>Ground turkey – 1 lb.</li><li>Fresh kale leaves – 1 C. trimmed and finely cut up</li><li>Onion – 1 C. cut up</li><li>Chopped green chilies – 1 (4 oz.) can</li><li>Garlic cloves – 2, finely cut up</li><li>Egg – 1, whisked</li><li>Fresh breadcrumbs – ½ C.</li><li>Monterey Jack cheese– 1 C. grated</li><li>Salsa verde – ¼ C.</li><li>Fresh cilantro – 3 tbsp. cut up</li><li>Red chili powder – 1 tsp.</li><li>Powdered cumin – ½ tsp.</li><li>Dried oregano – ½ tsp. crushed</li><li>Salt and powdered black pepper, as desired</li></ul>	<ul><li>Boneless chicken breasts – 4 (4 oz.)</li><li>Sausages – 4, casing removed</li></ul>

Method of Cooking:

1. For the meatloaf, put ground turkey and remnant ingredients into a deep bowl and, with your hands, mix to incorporate thoroughly.
2. Divide the turkey mixture into 4 portions and shape each into a mini loaf.
3. To turn on the 2-Basket Air Fryer, press "Power".
4. Then press "Start/Pause" to start cooking.
5. Spray the basket of "Zone 1".
6. Press "Zone 1" and choose "Air Fry".
7. Press "Temp" to adjust to 400°F and then press "Time" for 5 minutes to preheat.
8. After preheating, lay out the loaves into the "Zone 1" basket.
9. Slide the basket into the Air Fryer and press "Time" to adjust for 20 minutes.
10. After cooking time is finished, press "Start/Pause" to stop cooking.
11. Meanwhile, for the chicken breasts, lay out the chicken breasts on a smooth counter and, with a meat mallet, pound each into an even thickness.
12. Place 1 sausage over each chicken breast.
13. Roll each breast around the sausage and secure it with toothpicks.

14. Spray the basket of "Zone 2".
15. Press "Zone 2" and choose "Air Fry".
16. Press "Temp" to adjust to 375°F and then press "Time" for 5 minutes to preheat.
17. After preheating, lay the chicken breasts in the "Zone 2" basket.
18. Slide the basket into the Air Fryer and press "Time" to adjust for 15 minutes.
19. After cooking time is finished, press "Start/Pause" to stop cooking.
20. Take out the loaves and chicken breasts from the Air Fryer and enjoy moderately hot.

Meat Recipes

Seasoned Pork Tenderloin + Beef Casserole

Cooking period: 45 mins. | Serving portions: 5

Seasoned Pork Tenderloin: Per Serving: Calories: 195, Carbs: 0g, Fat 4.8g, Protein 35.6g

Beef Casserole: Per Serving: Calories 412, Carbs: 6.3g, Fat 16.5g, Protein 56.4g

For the Seasoned Pork Tenderloin:	For the Beef Casserole:
<ul><li>Pork tenderloin – 1½ lb.</li><li>BBQ pork seasoning – 2-3 tbsp.</li><li>Salt and powdered black pepper, as desired</li></ul>	<ul><li>Ground beef – 2 lb.</li><li>Taco seasoning – 2 tbsp.</li><li>Cheddar cheese – 1 C. shredded</li><li>Cottage cheese – 1 C.</li><li>Salsa – 1 C.</li></ul>

Method of Cooking:

1. For the pork: rub the pork tenderloin with seasoning.
2. Spray the basket of "Zone 1".
3. Press "Zone 1" and choose "Roast".
4. Press "Temp" to adjust to 360°F and then press "Time" for 5 minutes to preheat.
5. After preheating, lay the pork tenderloin in the "Zone 1" basket.
6. Slide the basket into the Air Fryer and press "Time" to adjust for 45 minutes.
7. Put the beef and taco seasoning into a basin and stir to incorporate thoroughly.
8. Put in cheeses and salsa and stir to incorporate.
9. Place the mixture into a baking pan.
10. To turn on the 2-Basket Air Fryer, press "Power".
11. Then press "Start/Pause" to start cooking.
12. Press "Zone 2" and choose "Air Fry".
13. Press "Temp" to adjust to 370°F and then press "Time" for 5 minutes to preheat.
14. After preheating, lay the baking pan into the "Zone 2" basket.
15. Slide the basket into the Air Fryer and press "Time" to adjust for 25 minutes.
16. After cooking time is finished, press "Start/Pause" to stop cooking.
17. Take out the pork tenderloin and baking pan from the Air Fryer.
18. Place the pork tenderloin onto a platter for around 10 minutes.
19. Enjoy beef casserole moderately hot.
20. Cut the pork tenderloin into serving portions and enjoy.

Glazed Skirt Steak + Glazed Ham

Cooking period: 40 mins. | Serving portions: 4 |

Glazed Skirt Steak: Per Serving: Calories 421, Carbs 14g, Fat 21.4g, Protein 40.2g

Glazed Ham: Per Serving: Calories 477, Carbs 15.9 g, Fat 16.2g, Protein 31.2g

For the Glazed Skirt Steak:	For the Glazed Ham:
<ul><li>Skirt steak – 1¼ lb.</li><li>Soy sauce – ½ C.</li><li>White wine – ¼ C.</li><li>Lemon juice – 3-4 tbsp.</li><li>Sesame oil – 2 tbsp.</li><li>Maple syrup – 3 tbsp.</li><li>Red pepper flakes – 1 tbsp. crushed</li><li>Garlic cloves – 2, finely cut up</li></ul>	<ul><li>Ham – 1 lb. 10½ oz.</li><li>Whiskey – 1 C.</li><li>French mustard – 2 tbsp.</li><li>Honey – 2 tbsp.</li></ul>

Method of Cooking:

1. Put steak and remnant ingredients, except for the scallions, into a large-sized resealable bag.
2. Seal the bag and shake to incorporate thoroughly.
3. Place into your refrigerator for up to 2 hours.
4. Remove the steak from the bag and put it at room temperature for 20 minutes before cooking.
5. Place the skirt steak onto a greased baking pan.
6. To turn on the 2-Basket Air Fryer, press "Power".
7. Then press "Start/Pause" to start cooking.
8. Press "Zone 1" and choose "Bake".
9. Press "Temp" to adjust to 400⁰F and then press "Time" for 5 minutes to preheat.
10. After preheating, lay the baking pan into the "Zone 1" basket.
11. Slide the basket into the Air Fryer and press "Time" to adjust for 10 minutes.
12. After cooking time is finished, press "Start/Pause" to stop cooking.
13. For the ham: Place the ham at room temperature for around 30 minutes before cooking.
14. Put whiskey, mustard, and honey into a basin and stir to incorporate.
15. Place the ham into a baking pan with half of the honey mixture and coat well.
16. Press "Zone 2" and choose "Air Fry".
17. Press "Temp" to adjust to 320⁰F and then press "Time" to adjust for 5 minutes to preheat.
18. After preheating, lay the baking pan into the "Zone 2" basket.
19. Slide the basket into the Air Fryer and press "Time" to adjust for 40 minutes.
20. After 15 minutes, change the side of the ham and top with remnant honey mixture.
21. After cooking time is finished, press "Start/Pause" to stop cooking.
22. Take the steak and ham from the Air Fryer and place onto a chopping board for 10-15 minutes.
23. Cut the steak and ham into serving portions and enjoy.

Herbed Beef Roast + Glazed Pork Ribs

Cooking period: 45 mins. | Serving portions: 6 |

Herbed Beef Roast: Per Serving: Calories 362, Carbs 0.3g, Fat 14.2g, Protein 55.1g

Glazed Pork Ribs: Per Serving: Calories 457, Carbs 11.3g, Fat 26.9 g, Protein 40.7g

For the Herbed Beef Roast:	For the Glazed Pork Ribs:
• Olive oil – 1 tbsp. • Dried rosemary – 1 tsp. crushed • Dried thyme – 1 tsp. crushed • Salt, as desired	• Tomato sauce – ¾ C. • Honey – 3 tbsp. • Worcestershire sauce – 1 tbsp. • Soy sauce – 1 tbsp. • Lime juice – 1 tbsp. • Garlic powder – ½ tsp. • Red pepper flakes – ½ tsp. crushed • Powdered black pepper, as desired • Pork ribs – 2 lb.

Method of Cooking:

1. For the beef roast, put oil, herbs, and salt into a basin and stir to incorporate thoroughly.
2. Coat the roast with herb mixture.
3. To turn on the 2-Basket Air Fryer, press "Power".
4. Then press "Start/Pause" to start cooking.
5. Spray the basket of "Zone 1".
6. Press "Zone 1" and choose "Air Fry".
7. Press "Temp" to adjust to 360°F and then press "Time" to adjust for 5 minutes to preheat.
8. After preheating, lay the beef roast into the "Zone 1" basket.
9. Slide the basket into the Air Fryer and press "Time" to adjust for 45 minutes.
10. Meanwhile, put tomato sauce and remnant ingredients except pork ribs into a large-sized basin for the pork ribs and mix to incorporate thoroughly.
11. Put in pork ribs and coat with the mixture.
12. Spray the basket of "Zone 2". Press "Zone 2" and choose "Air Fry".
13. Press "Temp" to adjust to 355°F and then press "Time" for 5 minutes to preheat.
14. After preheating, lay the pork ribs in the "Zone 2" basket.
15. Slide the basket into the Air Fryer and press "Time" to adjust for 13 minutes.
16. After 7 minutes of cooking, change the side of the ribs.
17. After cooking time is finished, press "Start/Pause" to stop cooking.
18. Take out the roast and ribs from the Air Fryer.
19. Enjoy the ribs hot.
20. Move the roast onto a chopping board for around 10 minutes.
21. Cut the beef roast into serving portions and enjoy.

Pineapple Lamb Chops + Glazed Pork Tenderloin

Cooking period: 40 mins. | Serving portions: 3

Pineapple Lamb Chops: Per Serving: Calories 405, Carbs 16.3g, Fat 18.1g, Protein 44.3g

Glazed Pork Tenderloin: Per Serving: Calories 264, Carbs 12.5g, Fat 5.6g, Protein 39.7g

For the Pineapple Lamb Chops:	For the Glazed Pork Tenderloin:
• Lamb shoulder chops – – 3 (8-oz.) • Salt and powdered black pepper, as desired • Brown sugar – ¼ C. • Pineapple slices – 4-5 • Pineapple juice – ¼-½ C.	• Red hot sauce – 2 tbsp. • Honey – 2 tbsp. • Fresh rosemary – 1 tbsp. finely cut up • Red pepper flakes – ¼ tsp. crushed • Salt, as desired • Pork tenderloin – 1 lb.

Method of Cooking:

1. For the chops rub the chops with salt and pepper.
2. Lay the chops into a baking pan and top with the brown sugar, pineapple slices, and juice.
3. To turn on the 2-Basket Air Fryer, press "Power".
4. Then press "Start/Pause" to start cooking.
5. Press "Zone 1" and choose "Bake".
6. Press "Temp" to adjust to 375°F and then press "Time" for 5 minutes to preheat.
7. After preheating, lay the chops in the "Zone 1" basket.
8. Slide the basket into the Air Fryer and press "Time" to adjust for 40 minutes.
9. After 20 minutes of cooking, baste the chops with juices.
10. Meanwhile, for the pork tenderloin, put the hot sauce, honey, rosemary, red pepper flakes, and salt into a small basin and stir to incorporate thoroughly.
11. Brush the pork tenderloin with the mixture.
12. Spray the basket of "Zone 2".
13. Press "Zone 2" and choose "Air Fry".
14. Press "Temp" to adjust to 350°F and then press "Time" for 5 minutes to preheat.
15. After preheating, lay the pork tenderloin into the "Zone 2" basket.
16. Slide the basket into the Air Fryer and press "Time" to adjust for 20 minutes.
17. After cooking time is finished, press "Start/Pause" to stop cooking.
18. Take out the pork tenderloin and chops from the Air Fryer.
19. Enjoy the chops hot alongside the pineapple slices.
20. Place the pork tenderloin onto a chopping board for around 10 minutes.
21. Cut the tenderloin into serving portions and enjoy.

Breaded Pork Chops + Seasoned Rib-Eye Steak

Cooking period: 15 mins. | Serving portions: 3

Breaded Pork Chops: Per Serving: Calories 413, Carbs 31g, Fat 20.2g, Protein 28.3g

Seasoned Rib-Eye Steak: Per Serving: Calories 495, Carbs 0g, Fat 42.8g, Protein 26.8g

For the Breaded Pork Chops:	For the Seasoned Rib-Eye Steak:
• Pork chops – – 3 (6-oz.) • Salt and powdered black pepper, as desired • Plain flour – ¼ C. • Egg – 1 • Seasoned breadcrumbs – 4 oz. • Canola oil – 1 tbsp.	• Rib-eye steaks – – 2 (8-oz.) • Olive oil – 2 tbsp. • Steak seasoning – 1 tbsp. • Salt and powdered black pepper, as desired

Method of Cooking:

1. Rub each pork chop with salt and pepper.
2. Put the flour into a shallow basin.
3. Put the egg into a second shallow basin and whisk thoroughly.
4. Put the breadcrumbs and oil into a third shallow basin and mix into a crumbly mixture.
5. Coat the pork chops with flour, dip into whisked egg, and coat with the breadcrumb mixture.
6. To turn on the 2-Basket Air Fryer, press "Power".
7. Then press "Start/Pause" to start cooking.
8. Spray the basket of "Zone 1".
9. Press "Zone 1" and choose "Air Fry".
10. Press "Temp" to adjust to 400°F and then press "Time" for 5 minutes to preheat.
11. After preheating, lay the pork chops in the "Zone 1" basket.
12. Slide the basket into the Air Fryer and press "Time" to adjust for 15 minutes.
13. Change the side of the chops once halfway through.
14. Meanwhile, for the steak, coat the steaks with oil and then sprinkle with seasoning, salt, and pepper.
15. Spray the basket of "Zone 2".
16. Press "Zone 2" and choose "Bake".
17. Press "Temp" to adjust to 400°F and then press "Time" for 5 minutes to preheat.
18. After preheating, lay the steaks into the "Zone 2" basket.
19. Slide the basket into the Air Fryer and press "Time" to adjust for 14 minutes.
20. After cooking time is finished, press "Start/Pause" to stop cooking.
21. Take off the chops and steaks from the Air Fryer.
22. Place the steaks onto a chopping board for around 5 minutes.
23. Enjoy the pork chops hot.
24. Cut each steak into serving portions and enjoy.

Rosemary Leg of Lamb + Seasoned Pork Shoulder

Cooking period: 1 hr. 40 mins. | Serving portions: 10

Rosemary Leg of Lamb: Per Serving: Calories 401, Carbs 4.3g, Fat 18.8g, Protein 51.3g

Seasoned Pork Shoulder: Per Serving: Calories 397, Carbs 0g, Fat 29.1g, Protein 31.7g

For the Rosemary Leg of Lamb:	For the Seasoned Pork Shoulder:
<ul><li>Olive oil – ¼ C.</li><li>Garlic cloves – 4, cut up</li><li>Fresh rosemary – ¼ C.</li><li>Dijon mustard – 3 tbsp.</li><li>Maple syrup – 2 tbsp.</li><li>Salt and powdered black pepper, as desired</li><li>Leg of lamb – 1 (4 lb.)</li></ul>	<ul><li>Skin-on, bone-in pork shoulder – 3 lb.</li><li>Adobo seasoning – 2-3 tbsp.</li><li>Salt, as desired</li></ul>

Method of Cooking:

1. For the leg of lamb, put the oil, garlic, herbs, mustard, honey, salt, and pepper into a food mixer and process to form a smooth mixture.
2. Place the leg of lamb and marinade into a glass baking pan and mix to incorporate thoroughly.
3. Cover the baking pan with cling film and place it into your refrigerator to marinate for 6-8 hours.
4. To turn on the 2-Basket Air Fryer, press "Power".
5. Then press "Start/Pause" to start cooking.
6. Spray the basket of "Zone 1". Press "Zone 1" and choose "Bake".
7. Press "Temp" to adjust to 420°F and then press "Time" for 5 minutes to preheat.
8. After preheating, lay out the leg of lamb into the "Zone 1" basket.
9. Slide the basket into the Air Fryer and press "Time" to adjust for 20 minutes.
10. After 20 minutes of cooking, Press "Temp" to adjust to 320°F and then press "Time" to adjust for 1 hour and 20 minutes.
11. Meanwhile, for the pork shoulder, lay out the pork shoulder on a chopping board, skin-side down.
12. Rub the inner side of the pork shoulder with adobo seasoning and salt.
13. Tie the pork shoulder with kitchen twines into a long round cylinder shape.
14. Rub the outer side of the pork shoulder with salt.
15. Spray the basket of "Zone 2". Press "Zone 2" and choose "Roast".
16. Press "Temp" to adjust to 350°F and then press "Time" to adjust for 5 minutes to preheat.
17. After preheating, lay the pork shoulder in the "Zone 2" basket.
18. Slide the basket into the Air Fryer and press "Time" to adjust for 60 minutes.
19. After cooking time is finished, press "Start/Pause" to stop cooking.
20. Take out the leg of lamb and pork shoulder from the Air Fryer and place onto a chopping board.
21. Cover the leg of lamb and pork shoulder for around 10-15 minutes with a piece of heavy-duty foil.
22. Cut the leg of lamb and pork shoulder into serving portions and enjoy.

BBQ Beef Ribs + Herbed Pork Loin

Cooking period: 25 mins. | Serving portions: 6

BBQ Beef Ribs: Per Serving: Calories 362, Carbs 18.3g, Fat 24.4g, Protein 18.1g

Herbed Pork Loin: Per Serving: Calories 391, Carbs 6.6g, Fat 21.1g, Protein 41.4g

For the BBQ Beef Ribs:	For the Herbed Pork Loin:
<ul><li>Boneless beef ribs – 2 lb.</li><li>Paprika – 1 tsp.</li><li>Garlic powder – ½ tsp.</li><li>Onion powder – ¼ tsp.</li><li>Salt and powdered black pepper, as desired</li><li>BBQ sauce – ½ C.</li><li>Liquid smoke – 1 tsp.</li><li>Brown sugar – 2 tbsp.</li></ul>	<ul><li>White sugar – 3 tbsp.</li><li>Dried basil – 1 tsp.</li><li>Dried thyme – 1 tsp.</li><li>Dried rosemary – 1 tsp.</li><li>Garlic powder – 1 tsp.</li><li>Salt and powdered black pepper, as desired</li><li>Pork loin – 2 lb.</li></ul>

Method of Cooking:

1. Put spices, salt, and pepper into a small basin for the beef ribs and mix to incorporate.
2. Rub the ribs with a spice mixture.
3. To turn on the 2-Basket Air Fryer, press "Power". Then press "Start/Pause" to start cooking.
4. Spray the basket of "Zone 1". Press "Zone 1" and choose "Air Fry".
5. Press "Temp" to adjust to 380⁰F and then press "Time" for 5 minutes to preheat.
6. After preheating, lay the ribs in the "Zone 1" basket.
7. Slide the basket into the Air Fryer and press "Time" for 15 minutes.
8. After 8 minutes of cooking, change the side of the ribs.
9. Meanwhile, put BBQ sauce, liquid smoke, and brown sugar into a basin and stir to incorporate.
10. After 15 minutes of cooking, coat the ribs with the sauce mixture.
11. Press "Temp" to adjust to 400⁰F and then press "Time" to adjust for 10 minutes.
12. Meanwhile, put the sugar, herbs, garlic powder, salt, and pepper into a basin for the pork and stir to incorporate thoroughly. Rub the pork loin with the herb mixture.
13. Spray the basket of "Zone 2". Press "Zone 2" and choose "Air Fry".
14. Press "Temp" to adjust to 400⁰F and then press "Time" for 5 minutes to preheat.
15. After preheating, lay the pork loin into the "Zone 2" basket.
16. Slide the basket into the Air Fryer and press "Time" to adjust for 20 minutes.
17. After cooking time is finished, press "Start/Pause" to stop cooking.
18. Take out the ribs and pork loin from the Air Fryer.
19. Place the ribs into the bowl with the remnant sauce mixture and mix to incorporate.
20. Enjoy the ribs immediately.
21. Place the pork loin onto a chopping board for around 10 minutes.
22. Cut the loin into serving portions and enjoy.

Stuffed Pork Roll + Bacon-Wrapped Beef Tenderloins

Cooking period: 15 mins. | Serving portions: 4

Stuffed Pork Roll: Per Serving: Calories 447, Carbs 20.3g, Fat 21g, Protein 43.9 g

Bacon-Wrapped Beef Tenderloin: Per Serving: Calories 841, Carbs 0.8g, Fat 52g, Protein 87.1g

For the Stuffed Pork Roll:	For the Bacon-Wrapped Beef Tenderloin:
<ul><li>Scallion – 1, cut up</li><li>Sun-dried tomatoes – ¼ C. finely cut up</li><li>Fresh parsley – 2 tbsp. cut up</li><li>Salt and powdered black pepper, as desired</li><li>Pork cutlets – 4 (6 oz.), pounded slightly</li><li>Paprika – 2 tsp.</li><li>Olive oil – ½ tbsp.</li></ul>	<ul><li>Bacon strips – 8</li><li>Center-cut beef tenderloin fillets – 4 (8 oz.)</li><li>Olive oil – 2 tbsp. divided</li><li>Salt and powdered black pepper, as desired</li></ul>

Method of Cooking:

1. For the pork, put scallion, tomatoes, parsley, salt, and pepper into a basin and stir to incorporate.
2. Coat each cutlet with tomato mixture.
3. Roll each cutlet and secure it with cocktail sticks.
4. Rub the outer part of the rolls with paprika, salt and pepper.
5. Coat the rolls with oil.
6. To turn on the 2-Basket Air Fryer, press "Power".
7. Then press "Start/Pause" to start cooking.
8. Spray the basket of "Zone 1".
9. Press "Zone 1" and choose "Air Fry".
10. Press "Temp" to adjust to 390°F and then press "Time" for 5 minutes to preheat.
11. After preheating, lay the pork rolls into the "Zone 1" basket.
12. Slide the basket into the Air Fryer and press "Time" to adjust for 15 minutes.
13. After 8 minutes of cooking, change the side of the pork rolls.
14. Meanwhile, for the beef, wrap 2 bacon strips around the entire outside of each beef filet.
15. With toothpicks, secure each filet.
16. Coat each wrapped filet with oil and sprinkle with salt and pepper.
17. Spray the basket of "Zone 2".
18. Press "Zone 2" and choose "Air Broil".
19. Press "Time" to adjust for 5 minutes to preheat.
20. After preheating, lay the wrapped filets into the "Zone 2" basket.
21. Slide the basket into the Air Fryer and press "Time" to adjust for 12 minutes.
22. After 6 minutes of cooking, change the side of the filets.
23. After cooking time is finished, press "Start/Pause" to stop cooking.
24. Place the pork rolls and fillets onto a platter for 10 minutes before enjoying. Enjoy hot.

Spiced Pork Shoulder + Glazed Beef Short Ribs

Cooking period: 55 mins. | Serving portions: 6

Spiced Pork Shoulder: Per Serving: Calories 445, Carbs 0.7g, Fat 32.5g, Protein 35.4g

Glazed Beef Short Ribs: Per Serving: Calories 333, Carbs 4.1g, Fat 13.7g, Protein 45.1g

For the Spiced Pork Shoulder:	For the Glazed Beef Short Ribs:
<ul><li>Powdered cumin – 1 tsp.</li><li>Cayenne pepper powder – 1 tsp.</li><li>Garlic powder – 1 tsp.</li><li>Salt and powdered black pepper, as desired.</li><li>Skin-on pork shoulder – 2 lb.</li></ul>	<ul><li>Bone-in beef short ribs – 2 lb.</li><li>Scallions – 3 tbsp. cut up</li><li>Fresh ginger – ½ tbsp. finely grated</li><li>Soy sauce – ½ C.</li><li>Balsamic vinegar – ¼ C.</li><li>Sriracha – ½ tbsp.</li><li>Brown sugar – 1 tbsp.</li><li>Powdered black pepper – ½ tsp.</li></ul>

Method of Cooking:

1. For the pork, put spices, salt, and pepper into a small basin and mix to incorporate.
2. Rub the pork shoulder with the spice mixture.
3. Tie the pork shoulder with kitchen twines into a long round cylinder shape.
4. To turn on the 2-Basket Air Fryer, press "Power".
5. Then press "Start/Pause" to start cooking.
6. Spray the basket of "Zone 1". Press "Zone 1" and choose "Roast".
7. Press "Temp" to adjust to 350°F and then press "Time" for 5 minutes to preheat.
8. After preheating, lay the shoulder into the "Zone 1" basket.
9. Slide the basket into the Air Fryer and press "Time" to adjust for 55 minutes.
10. Meanwhile, for the beef ribs, put the ribs and remnant ingredients into a resealable bag.
11. Seal the bag and shake to mix thoroughly.
12. Place into your refrigerator overnight.
13. Spray the basket of "Zone 2". Press "Zone 2" and choose "Air Fry".
14. Press "Temp" to adjust to 380°F and then press "Time" for 5 minutes to preheat.
15. After preheating, lay the ribs into the "Zone 2" basket.
16. Slide the basket into the Air Fryer and press "Time" to adjust for 8 minutes.
17. Change the side of the ribs once halfway through.
18. After cooking time is finished, press "Start/Pause" to stop cooking.
19. Take out the ribs and pork shoulder from the Air Fryer.
20. Move the pork shoulder onto a chopping board for around 10 minutes.
21. Enjoy the ribs hot.
22. Cut the pork shoulder into serving portions and enjoy.

Pistachio Crusted Rack of Lamb + Simple Pork Chops

Cooking period: 19 mins. | Serving portions: 4

Pistachio Crusted Rack of Lamb: Per Serving: Calories 824, Carbs 10.3g, Fat 39.3g, Protein 72g

Simple Pork Chops: Per Serving: Calories 544, Carbs 0g, Fat 24.3g, Protein 38.2g

For the Pistachio Crusted Rack of Lamb:	For the Simple Pork Chops:
<ul><li>Rack of lamb – 1, trimmed all fat and frenched</li><li>Salt and powdered black pepper, as desired</li><li>Pistachios – 1/3 C. finely cut up</li><li>Panko breadcrumbs – 2 tbsp.</li><li>Fresh thyme – 2 tsp. finely cut up</li><li>Fresh rosemary – 1 tsp. finely cut up</li><li>Unsalted butter – 1 tbsp. liquefied</li><li>Dijon mustard – 1 tbsp.</li></ul>	<ul><li>Pork chops – 4 (6-oz.) (½-inch thick)</li><li>Dried basil – ½ tsp. crushed</li><li>Salt and powdered black pepper, as desired</li></ul>

Method of Cooking:

1. For the lamb, rub the rack with salt and pepper.
2. To turn on the 2-Basket Air Fryer, press "Power".
3. Then press "Start/Pause" to start cooking.
4. Spray the basket of "Zone 1". Press "Zone 1" and choose "Air Fry".
5. Press "Temp" to adjust to 380°F and then press "Time" for 5 minutes to preheat.
6. After preheating, lay out the rack of lamb into the "Zone 1" basket.
7. Slide the basket into the Air Fryer and press "Time" to adjust for 12 minutes.
8. Meanwhile, put remnant ingredients except the mustard into a small basin and stir to incorporate.
9. After 12 minutes of cooking, brush the meaty side with the mustard.
10. Then, coat the pistachio mixture on all sides of the rack and press firmly.
11. Press "Time" to adjust for 7 minutes.
12. Meanwhile, for the pork chops, rub the pork chops with thyme, salt and pepper.
13. Spray the basket of "Zone 2". Press "Zone 2" and choose "Air Broil".
14. Press "Time" to adjust for 5 minutes to preheat.
15. After preheating, lay the pork chops in the "Zone 2" basket.
16. Slide the basket into the Air Fryer and press "Time" to adjust for 18 minutes.
17. Change the side of the chops after 12 minutes of cooking.
18. After cooking time is finished, press "Start/Pause" to stop cooking.
19. Take out the rack of lamb and pork chops from the Air Fryer.
20. Move the rack of lamb onto a chopping board for at least 10 minutes.
21. Enjoy the pork chops immediately.
22. Cut the rack into individual chops and enjoy.

Vegetable Recipes

Stuffed Pumpkin + Buttered Veggies

Cooking period: 30 mins. | Serving portions: 4 |

Stuffed Pumpkin: Per Serving: Calories 157, Carbs 35.9g, Fat 1.1g, Protein 4.6g

Buttered Veggies: Per Serving: Calories 183, Carbs 21.2g, Fat 10.7g, Protein 2.6g

For the Stuffed Pumpkin:	For the Buttered Veggies:
<ul><li>Sweet potato – 1, peel removed and cut up</li><li>Parsnip – 1, peel removed and cut up</li><li>Carrot – 1, peel removed and cut up</li><li>Fresh green peas – ½ C. shelled</li><li>Onion – 1, cut up</li><li>Garlic cloves – 2, finely cut up</li><li>Egg – 1, whisked</li><li>Mixed dried herbs – 2 tsp.</li><li>Salt and powdered black pepper, as desired</li><li>Butternut pumpkin – ½, seeds removed</li></ul>	<ul><li>Potatoes – 2 C. cut up</li><li>Beets – 1¼ C. peel removed and cut up</li><li>Carrots – 1¼ C. peel removed and cut up</li><li>Garlic cloves – 3, finely cut up</li><li>Salt and powdered black pepper, as desired</li><li>Olive oil – 3 tbsp.</li></ul>

Method of Cooking:

1. For the stuffed pumpkin, put vegetables, garlic, egg, herbs, salt, and pepper into a large-sized basin and stir to incorporate. Stuff the pumpkin half with vegetable mixture.
2. To turn on the 2-Basket Air Fryer, press "Power". Then press "Start/Pause" to start cooking.
3. Spray the basket of "Zone 1". Press "Zone 1" and choose "Air Fry".
4. Press "Temp" to adjust to 355⁰F and then press "Time" for 5 minutes to preheat.
5. After preheating, lay the pumpkin half into the "Zone 1" basket.
6. Slide the basket into the Air Fryer and press "Time" to adjust for 30 minutes.
7. Meanwhile, for the veggies, put potatoes and remnant ingredients in a bowl and toss to incorporate thoroughly.
8. Spray the basket of "Zone 2". Press "Zone 2" and choose "Bake".
9. Press "Temp" to adjust to 450⁰ and then press "Time" for 5 minutes to preheat.
10. After preheating, lay the veggie mixture in the "Zone 2" basket.
11. Slide the basket into the Air Fryer and press "Time" to adjust for 20 minutes.
12. Toss the veggie mixture once halfway through.
13. After cooking time is finished, press "Start/Pause" to stop cooking.
14. Take out pumpkin and veggies from the Air Fryer.
15. Place the pumpkin and veggies onto serving platters and let them cool slightly. Enjoy moderately hot.

Stuffed Zucchini + Mushroom with Green Peas

Cooking period: 35 mins. │Serving portions: 4 │

Stuffed Zucchini: Per Serving: Calories 181, Carbs 10.1g, Fat 11.6g, Protein 11.3g

Mushroom with Green Peas: Per Serving: Calories 132, Carbs 25g, Fat 0.3g, Protein 6.1g

For the Stuffed Zucchini:	For the Mushroom with Green Peas:
• Zucchinis – 2, cut in half lengthwise • Garlic powder – ½ tsp. • Salt, as desired • Olive oil – 1 tsp. • Fresh mushrooms – 4 oz. cut up • Carrots – 4 oz. peel removed and shredded • Onion – 3 oz. cut up • Goat cheese – 4 oz. crumbled • Fresh basil leaves – 12 • Onion powder – ½ tsp.	• Soy sauce – ½ C. • Maple syrup – 4 tbsp. • Rice vinegar – 4 tbsp. • Garlic cloves – 4, finely cut up • Chinese five spice powder – 2 tsp. • Powdered ginger – ½ tsp. • Fresh Cremini mushrooms – 16 oz. halved • Frozen green peas – ½ C.

Method of Cooking:

1. For the zucchini: carefully scoop the flesh from the middle of each zucchini half.
2. Rub each zucchini half with a little garlic powder and salt.
3. To turn on the 2-Basket Air Fryer, press "Power". Then press "Start/Pause" to start cooking.
4. Spray the basket of "Zone 1". Press "Zone 1" and choose "Bake".
5. Press "Temp" to adjust to 450°F and then press "Time" for 5 minutes to preheat.
6. After preheating, lay out the zucchini halves into the "Zone 1" basket.
7. Slide the basket into the Air Fryer and press "Time" to adjust for 35 minutes.
8. Meanwhile, sizzle the oil in a wok on a burner at around medium heat.
9. Cook the mushrooms, carrots, onions, onion powder and salt. Cook for around 5-6 minutes.
10. Take off the burner and put it aside.
11. After 20 minutes of cooking, stuff each zucchini half with the veggie mixture and top with basil leaves, followed by the cheese.
12. Meanwhile, for the mushrooms with green peas, put soy sauce, maple syrup, vinegar, garlic, five-spice powder, and powdered ginger into a basin mix to incorporate thoroughly. Put it aside.
13. Place the mushroom into a greased baking pan.
14. Press "Zone 2" and choose "Air Fry". Press "Temp" to adjust to 350°F and then press "Time" for 5 minutes to preheat. After preheating, lay the baking pan into the "Zone 2" basket.
15. Slide the basket into the Air Fryer and press "Time" to adjust for 15 minutes.
16. After 10 minutes of cooking, put the peas and vinegar mixture in the pan with mushrooms and mix to incorporate. After cooking time is finished, press "Start/Pause" to stop cooking.
17. Take out the zucchini halves and pan of veggies from the Air Fryer. Enjoy moderate hot.

Stuffed Eggplant + Brussels Sprout Salad

Cooking period: 25 mins. | Serving portions: 4

Stuffed Eggplants: Per Serving: Calories: 192, Carbs 33.8g, Fat 6.1g, Protein 6.9g

Brussels Sprout Salad: Per Serving: Calories 235, Carbs 34.5g, Fat 11.3g, Protein 4.9 g

For the Stuffed Eggplants:	**For the Brussels Sprout Salad:**
	For the Salad:
• Large-sized eggplants – 2	• Medium-sized Brussels sprouts – 1 lb. trimmed and halved vertically
• Olive oil – 4 tsp. divided	• Olive oil – 3 tsp.
• Lemon juice – 4 tsp. divided	• Salt and powdered black pepper, as desired
• Cherry tomatoes – 16, quartered	• Apples – 2, cored and cut up
• Tomato salsa – 4 tbsp.	• Red onion – 1, slivered
• Fresh parsley – ½ tbsp.	• Lettuce 4 C. torn
• Salt and powdered black pepper, as desired	
	For the Dressing:
	• Olive oil – 2 tbsp.
	• Lemon juice – 2 tbsp.
	• Apple cider vinegar – 1 tbsp.
	• Maple syrup – 1 tbsp.
	• Dijon mustard – 1 tsp.
	• Salt and powdered black pepper, as desired

Method of Cooking:

1. For the eggplant: to turn on the 2-Basket Air Fryer, press "Power".
2. Then press "Start/Pause" to start cooking.
3. Spray the basket of "Zone 1".
4. Press "Zone 1" and choose "Air Fry".
5. Press "Temp" to adjust to 390°F and then press "Time" to adjust for 5 minutes to preheat.
6. After preheating, lay the eggplants in the "Zone 1" basket.
7. Slide the basket into the Air Fryer and press "Time" to adjust for 15 minutes.
8. Take out the eggplants from the Air Fryer and cut each in half lengthwise.
9. Drizzle the eggplant halves with 1 tsp. of oil.
10. Again, press "Zone 1" and choose "Air Fry".
11. Press "Temp" to adjust to 355°F.
12. Lay out the eggplant halves into the "Zone 1" basket.
13. Slide the basket into the Air Fryer and press "Time" to adjust for 10 minutes.

14. Meanwhile, for the salad, put the Brussels sprouts, oil, salt, and pepper into a basin and toss to incorporate thoroughly.
15. Spray the basket of "Zone 2".
16. Press "Zone 2" and choose "Air Fry".
17. Press "Temp" to adjust to 360°F and then press "Time" for 5 minutes to preheat.
18. After preheating, lay the Brussels sprouts into the "Zone 2" basket.
19. Slide the basket into the Air Fryer and press "Time" to adjust for 15 minutes.
20. Change the side of the Brussels sprouts once halfway through.
21. After cooking time is finished, press "Start/Pause" to stop cooking.
22. Take out eggplants from the Air Fryer and put them aside for around 5 minutes.
23. Move the Brussels sprouts onto a plate and put them aside to cool slightly.
24. Carefully scoop out the flesh, leaving about ¼-inch away from the edges.
25. Drizzle the eggplant halves with 1 tsp of lemon juice.
26. Put the eggplant flesh into a basin.
27. Put in tomatoes, salsa, parsley, salt, pepper, remnant oil, and lemon juice and stir to incorporate thoroughly.
28. Stuff the eggplant haves with the salsa mixture and enjoy.
29. Put Brussels sprouts, apples, onion, and lettuce into a salad dish and mix to incorporate.
30. For the dressing: Put oil and remnant ingredients into a small basin and whisk to incorporate thoroughly.
31. Place the dressing over the salad and gently mix to incorporate.
32. Enjoy immediately.

Vegetarian Loaf + Potato Salad

Cooking period: 1 hr. 40 mins. | Serving portions: 6

Vegetarian Loaf: Per Serving: Calories 229, Carbs 33.4g, Fat 5.1g, Protein 12.8g

Potato Salad: Per Serving: Calories 203, Carbs 27g, Fat 8.5g, Protein 6g

For the Vegetarian Loaf:	For the Potato Salad:
<ul><li>Vegetable broth – 1 (14½-oz.) can</li><li>Brown lentils – ¾ C. rinsed</li><li>Olive oil – 1 tbsp.</li><li>Carrots – 1¾ C. peel removed and shredded</li><li>Fresh mushrooms – 1 C. cut up</li><li>Onion – 1 C. cut up</li><li>Fresh parsley – 1 tbsp. finely cut up</li><li>Fresh basil – 1 tbsp. finely cut up</li><li>Cooked brown rice – ½ C.</li><li>Mozzarella cheese – 1 C. shredded</li><li>Large-sized egg – 1</li><li>Large-sized egg white – 1</li><li>Salt and powdered black pepper, as desired</li><li>Tomato paste – 2 tbsp.</li><li>Water – 2 tbsp.</li></ul>	<ul><li>Russet potatoes – 4</li><li>Vegetable oil – 1 tbsp.</li><li>Salt, as desired</li><li>Hard-boiled eggs – 3, peel removed and cut up</li><li>Celery – 1 C. cut up</li><li>Red onion – ½ C., cut up</li><li>Prepared mustard – 1 tbsp.</li><li>Celery salt – ¼ tsp.</li><li>Garlic salt – ¼ tsp.</li><li>Mayonnaise – ¼ C.</li></ul>

Method of Cooking:

1. For the loaf, put the broth into a medium-sized saucepan on a burner at medium-high heat.
2. Cook the broth until boiling.
3. Stir in the lentils.
4. Cook the mixture until boiling.
5. Immediately turn the heat to low.
6. Cook with a cover for around 30 minutes.
7. Take off the burner and put it aside to cool slightly.
8. Meanwhile, sizzle the oil into a large-sized wok on a burner at around medium heat.
9. Cook the carrots, mushrooms, and onion for around 10 minutes.
10. Stir in herbs and take off the burner.
11. Place the veggie mixture into a large-sized basin and put it aside to cool slightly.
12. After cooling, add the lentils, rice, cheese, egg, egg white, and seasonings, then stir to incorporate thoroughly.

13. Put the tomato paste and water into a small basin and stir to incorporate.
14. Place the mixture into a greased bakery paper-lined loaf pan and top with water mixture.
15. To turn on the 2-Basket Air Fryer, press "Power".
16. Then press "Start/Pause" to start cooking.
17. Spray the basket of "Zone 1".
18. Press "Zone 1" and choose "Bake".
19. Press "Temp" to adjust to 350°F and then press "Time" for 5 minutes to preheat.
20. After preheating, lay the loaf pan into the "Zone 1" basket.
21. Slide the basket into the Air Fryer and press "Time" to adjust for 50 minutes.
22. Meanwhile, for the salad, with a fork, prick the potatoes.
23. Drizzle the potatoes with oil and rub with the salt.
24. Spray the basket of "Zone 2".
25. Press "Zone 2" and choose "Air Fry".
26. Press "Temp" to adjust to 390°F and then press "Time" for 5 minutes to preheat.
27. After preheating, lay the potatoes in the "Zone 2" basket.
28. Slide the basket into the Air Fryer and press "Time" to adjust for 40 minutes.
29. After cooking time is finished, press "Start/Pause" to stop cooking.
30. Take out the loaf pan and potatoes from the Air Fryer.
31. Move the potatoes into a basin and put them aside to cool.
32. Put the loaf pan onto a counter for around 10 minutes before slicing.
33. Carefully turn the loaf onto a platter.
34. Cut into serving portions and enjoy.
35. After cooling, chop the potatoes.
36. Put the potatoes and remnant ingredients into a serving bowl and gently stir to incorporate.
37. Place into your refrigerator to chill before enjoying.

Potato Gratin + Ratatouille

Cooking period: 20 mins.　Serving portions: 4

Potato Gratin: Per Serving: Calories 233, Carbs 31.3g, Fat 8g, Protein 9.7

Ratatouille: Per Serving: Calories 119, Carbs 20.3g, Fat 4.2g, Protein 3.6g

For the Potato Gratin:	For the Ratatouille:
<ul><li>Large-sized potatoes – 2, slivered thinly</li><li>Cream – 5½ tbsp.</li><li>Eggs – 2</li><li>Plain flour – 1 tbsp.</li><li>Cheddar cheese – ½ C. grated</li></ul>	<ul><li>Bell peppers – 2, seeds removed and cut up</li><li>Eggplant – 1, cut up</li><li>Zucchini – 1, cut up</li><li>Tomatoes – 3, cut up</li><li>Small-sized onions 2, cut up</li><li>Garlic cloves – 2, finely cut up</li><li>Herbs de Provence – 2 tbsp.</li><li>Olive oil – 1 tbsp.</li><li>Balsamic vinegar – 1 tbsp.</li><li>Salt and powdered black pepper, as desired</li></ul>

Method of Cooking:

1. For the potato gratin: to turn on the 2-Basket Air Fryer, press "Power".
2. Then press "Start/Pause" to start cooking.
3. Spray the basket of "Zone 1". Press "Zone 1" and choose "Air Fry".
4. Press "Temp" to adjust to 355°F and then press "Time" to adjust for 5 minutes to preheat.
5. After preheating, lay the potato slices in the "Zone 1" basket.
6. Slide the basket into the Air Fryer and press "Time" to adjust for 10 minutes.
7. Meanwhile, put cream, eggs, and flour into a basin and stir to form a thick sauce.
8. Take out the potato slices from the Air Fryer.
9. Divide the potato slices into 4 ramekins and top with the egg mixture, followed by the cheese.
10. Again, press "Zone 1" and choose "Air Fry". Press "Temp" to adjust to 390°F.
11. Lay out the ramekins into the "Zone 1" basket.
12. Slide the basket into the Air Fryer and press "Time" to adjust for 10 minutes.
13. Meanwhile, for the ratatouille, put the vegetables, garlic, Herbs de Provence, oil, vinegar, salt, and pepper into a large basin and toss to incorporate thoroughly.
14. Spray the basket of "Zone 2".
15. Press "Zone 2" and choose "Air Fry".
16. Press "Temp" to adjust to 355°F and then press "Time" for 5 minutes to preheat.
17. After preheating, lay the vegetable mixture in the "Zone 2" basket.
18. Slide the basket into the Air Fryer and press "Time" to adjust for 15 minutes.
19. After the cooking time is finished, press "Start/Pause" to stop cooking.
20. Take out the vegetable mixture and ramekins from the Air Fryer and enjoy hot.

Dessert Recipes

Cherry Crumble + Chocolate Pudding

Cooking period: 25 mins. Serving portions: 4

Cherry Crumble: Per Serving: Calories 334, Carbs 55.2g, Fat 11.8g, Protein 2.3g

Chocolate Pudding: Per Serving: Calories 454, Carbs 34.2g, Fat 33.6g, Protein 5.7g

For the Cherry Crumble:	For the Chocolate Pudding:
<ul><li>Cherry pie filling – 1 (14-oz.) can</li><li>Unsalted butter – ¼ C. softened</li><li>Self-rising flour – 9 tbsp.</li><li>Caster sugar – 7 tbsp.</li><li>Salt – 1 pinch</li></ul>	<ul><li>Unsalted butter – ½ C.</li><li>Dark chocolate – 2/3 C. cut up</li><li>Caster sugar – ¼ C.</li><li>Medium-sized eggs – 2</li><li>Orange rind – 2 tsp. finely grated</li><li>Orange juice – ¼ C.</li><li>Self-rising flour – 2 tbsp.</li></ul>

Method of Cooking:

1. For the crumble, put the cherry pie filling into a lightly greased baking pan.
2. Put remnant ingredients into a medium-sized basin and rub until a crumbly mixture forms.
3. Spread the mixture over the cherry pie filling.
4. To turn on the 2-Basket Air Fryer, press "Power".
5. Then press "Start/Pause" to start cooking.
6. Press "Zone 1" and choose "Air Fry".
7. Press "Temp" to adjust to 320°F and then press "Time" for 5 minutes to preheat.
8. After preheating, lay the baking pan in the "Zone 1" basket.
9. Slide the basket into the Air Fryer and press "Time" to adjust for 25 minutes.
10. Meanwhile, put the butter and chocolate into a microwave-safe bowl for the chocolate pudding.
11. Microwave on high setting for around 2 minutes, stirring after every 30 seconds.
12. Take it out of the microwave and stir it to form a smooth mixture.
13. Put in sugar and eggs and whisk to form a frothy mixture.
14. Put in orange rind and juice, followed by flour, and stir to incorporate thoroughly.
15. Divide mixture into 4 greased ramekins about ¾ full.
16. Press "Zone 2" and choose "Air Fry".
17. Press "Temp" to adjust to 355°F and then press "Time" for 5 minutes to preheat.
18. After preheating, lay the ramekins in the "Zone 2" basket.
19. Slide the basket into the Air Fryer and press "Time" to adjust for 12 minutes.
20. After cooking time is finished, press "Start/Pause" to stop cooking.
21. Take out the baking pan and ramekins from the Air Fryer.
22. Enjoy moderately hot.

Chocolate Mug Cakes + Lava Cake

Cooking period: 17 mins. | Serving portions: 4

Chocolate Mug Cakes: Per Serving: Calories 409, Carbs 66g, Fat 14g, Protein 5.9g

Lava Cake: Per Serving: Calories 122, Carbs 5g, Fat 11g, Protein 4.6g

For Chocolate Mug Cakes:	For the Lava Cake:
• All-purpose flour – ½ C. • White sugar – 4 tbsp. • Baking powder – ½ tsp. • Baking soda – ¼ tsp. • Salt – 1/8 tsp. • Milk – 4 tbsp. • Applesauce – 4 tbsp. • Vegetable oil – 1 tbsp. • Vanilla extract – ½ tsp. • Chocolate chips – 4 tbsp.	• Egg – 1 • Unsweetened cocoa powder – 2 tbsp. • Golden flax meal – 1 tbsp. • Erythritol – 2 tbsp. • Stevia powder – 1/8 tsp. • Water – 2 tbsp. • Coconut oil – 1 tbsp. liquefied • Baking powder – ½ tsp. • Dash of vanilla extract • Salt – 1 pinch

Method of Cooking:

1. For the mug cakes: to turn on the 2-Basket Air Fryer, press "Power".
2. Then press "Start/Pause" to start cooking.
3. Press "Zone 1" and choose "Bake".
4. Press "Temp" to adjust to 375°F and then press "Time" for 5 minutes to preheat.
5. Put the all-purpose flour, sugar, baking powder, baking soda, and salt into a basin and stir to incorporate.
6. Put in milk, applesauce, oil, and vanilla extract and stir to incorporate thoroughly.
7. Lightly mix in the chocolate chips.
8. Divide the mixture into 2 heatproof mugs.
9. After preheating, lay the mugs in the "Zone 1" basket.
10. Slide the basket into the Air Fryer and press "Time" to adjust for 17 minutes.
11. Meanwhile, for the lava cake, put egg and remnant ingredients into a small glass Pyrex dish and whisk to incorporate thoroughly.
12. Press "Zone 2" and choose "Air Fry".
13. Press "Temp" to adjust to 350°F and then press "Time" for 5 minutes to preheat.
14. After preheating, lay the Pyrex dish into the "Zone 2" basket.
15. Slide the basket into the Air Fryer and press "Time" to adjust for 9 minutes.
16. After cooking time is finished, press "Start/Pause" to stop cooking.
17. Take out the mugs and Pyrex dish from the Air Fryer.
18. Enjoy moderately hot.

Apple Crumble + Glazed Figs

Cooking period: 25 mins. | Serving portions: 4

Apple Crumble: Per Serving: Calories 344, Carbs 60.3g, Fat 11.8g, Protein 2g

Glazed Figs: Per Serving: Calories 69, Carbs 17.9g, Fat 0.2g, Protein 0.7g

For the Apple Crumble:	For the Glazed Figs:
<ul><li>Apple pie filling – 1 (14-oz.) can</li><li>Unsalted butter – ¼ C. softened</li><li>Self-rising flour – 9 tbsp.</li><li>Caster sugar – 7 tbsp.</li><li>Salt – 1 pinch</li></ul>	<ul><li>Fresh figs – 4</li><li>Honey – 4 tsp.</li><li>Powdered cinnamon – 1 pinch</li></ul>

Method of Cooking:

1. Lightly grease a baking pan.
2. Place apple pie filling into the prepared baking pan.
3. Put remnant ingredients into a medium-sized basin and rub with fingers to form a crumbly mixture forms.
4. Spread the mixture over the apple pie filling.
5. To turn on the 2-Basket Air Fryer, press "Power".
6. Then press "Start/Pause" to start cooking.
7. Press "Zone 1" and choose "Air Fry".
8. Press "Temp" to adjust to 320°F and then press "Time" for 5 minutes to preheat.
9. After preheating, lay the baking pan into the "Zone 1" basket.
10. Slide the basket into the Air Fryer and press "Time" to adjust for 25 minutes.
11. Meanwhile, for the figs:
12. Cut each fig into quarters, leaving a little at the base to hold the fruit together.
13. Drizzle the figs with honey and sprinkle with cinnamon.
14. Spray the basket of "Zone 2".
15. Press "Zone 2" and choose "Air Broil".
16. Press "Time" to adjust for 5 minutes to preheat.
17. After preheating, lay the figs in the "Zone 2" basket.
18. Slide the basket into the Air Fryer and press "Time" to adjust for 15 minutes.
19. After cooking time is finished, press "Start/Pause" to stop cooking.
20. Take out the baking pan and figs from the Air Fryer.
21. Place the baking pan onto a counter to cool for around 10 minutes.
22. Enjoy the crumble and figs moderately hot.

Apple Bread Pudding + Cherry Clafoutis

Cooking period: 25 mins. Serving portions: 4

Apple Bread Pudding: Per Serving: Calories 416, Carbs 66.5g, Fat 14g, Protein 7.6g

Cherry Clafoutis: Per Serving: Calories 241, Carbs 29 g, Fat 10.1g, Protein 3.9 g

For the Apple Bread Pudding:	For the Cherry Clafoutis:
For the Bread Pudding: • Bread – 5¼ oz. cubed • Apple – ¼ C. peel removed, cored, and cut up • Raisins – ¼ C. • Almonds – 2 tbsp. cut up • Milk – ¾ C. • Water – 1/3 C. • Maple syrup – 2½ tbsp. • Powdered cinnamon – 1 tsp. • Cornstarch – 1 tsp. • Vanilla extract – 1 tsp. **For the Topping:** • Plain flour – ½ C. plus 3 tbsp. • Brown sugar – 4½ tbsp. • Unsalted butter – 3½ tbsp.	• Fresh cherries – 1½ C. pitted • Vodka – 3 tbsp. • All-purpose flour – ¼ C. • White sugar – 2 tbsp. • Salt – 1 pinch • Sour cream – ½ C. • Egg – 1 • Unsalted butter – 1 tbsp. • Powdered sugar – ¼ C.

Method of Cooking:

1. Put the bread, apple, raisins, and almonds into a large basin; stir to incorporate thoroughly.
2. Put remnant pudding ingredients into another basin and stir to incorporate thoroughly.
3. Put milk mixture into bread mixture and stir to incorporate thoroughly.
4. Place into your refrigerator for around 15 minutes, tossing occasionally.
5. For the topping, put flour and sugar into a basin and stir to incorporate.
6. With a pastry cutter, cut in the butter to form a crumbly mixture.
7. Place the mixture into a baking pan and spread the topping mixture on top.
8. To turn on the 2-Basket Air Fryer, press "Power".
9. Then press "Start/Pause" to start cooking.
10. Press "Zone 1" and choose "Air Fry".
11. Press "Temp" to adjust to 355ºF and then press "Time" for 5 minutes to preheat.
12. After preheating, lay the baking pan into the "Zone 1" basket.

13. Slide the basket into the Air Fryer and press "Time" to adjust for 22 minutes.
14. Meanwhile, for the Clafoutis, put cherries and vodka into a basin and stir to incorporate.
15. Put the flour, sugar, and salt into another basin and stir to incorporate thoroughly.
16. Put in sour cream and egg and mix to form a smooth dough.
17. Place the flour mixture into a greased cake pan.
18. Spread cherry mixture over the dough.
19. Now, put the butter on top in the form of dots.
20. Press "Zone 2" and choose "Air Fry".
21. Press "Temp" to adjust to 355°F and then press "Time" for 5 minutes to preheat.
22. After preheating, lay the cake pan in the "Zone 2" basket.
23. Slide the basket into the Air Fryer and press "Time" to adjust for 25 minutes.
24. After cooking time is finished, press "Start/Pause" to stop cooking.
25. Take out both pans from the Air Fryer.
26. Move both pans onto a counter to cool for around 10 minutes.
27. Carefully turn the Clafoutis onto a platter and sprinkle with powdered sugar.
28. Enjoy moderately hot.

White Chocolate Cheesecake + Rum Cake

Cooking period: 34 mins. | Serving portions: 6

White Chocolate Cheesecake: Per Serving: Calories 299, Carbs 29.8g, Fat 18.3g, Protein 6.3g

Rum Cake: Per Serving: Calories 315, Carbs 26.5g, Fat 14.9g, Protein 3.5g

For the Chocolate Cheesecake:	For the Rum Cake:
• Eggs – 3 (whites and yolks separated) • White chocolate – 1 C. cut up • Cream cheese – ½ C. softened • Unsweetened cocoa powder – 2 tbsp. • Powdered sugar – 2 tbsp. • Raspberry jam – ¼ C.	• Yellow cake mix – ½ package • Jell-O instant pudding – ½ (3.4-oz.) package • Eggs – 2 • Vegetable oil – ¼ C. • Water – ¼ C. • Dark rum – ¼ C

Method of Cooking:

1. Meanwhile, for cheesecake, put the egg whites into a basin and place into your refrigerator to chill before using.
2. Put the chocolate into a microwave-safe bowl and microwave on high power for around 2 minutes, stirring every 30 seconds.
3. Put the cream cheese into the bowl of chocolate and microwave for around 1-2 minutes, stirring every 30 seconds.
4. Take out from the microwave and stir in cocoa powder and egg yolks.
5. Take out the egg whites from the refrigerator and whisk to form firm peaks.
6. Add 1/3 of the mixed egg whites into the cheese mixture and lightly stir to incorporate.
7. Lightly mix in remnant egg whites.
8. Place the mixture into a 6-inch cake pan.
9. To turn on the 2-Basket Air Fryer, press "Power".
10. Then press "Start/Pause" to start cooking.
11. Press "Zone 2" and choose "Air Fry".
12. Press "Temp" to adjust to 285ºF and then press "Time" for 5 minutes to preheat.
13. After preheating, lay the cake pan in the "Zone 2" basket.
14. Slide the basket into the Air Fryer and press "Time" to adjust for 30 minutes.
15. Meanwhile, for the cake, put cake mix and remnant ingredients into a basin and, with an electric mixer, beat until well combined.
16. Lay out a bakery paper in the bottom of a greased cake pan.
17. Place the mixture into the prepared baking pan and smooth the top surface with the back of a spoon.
18. Press "Zone 2" and choose "Air Fry".
19. Press "Temp" to adjust to 325ºF and then press "Time" for 5 minutes to preheat.
20. After preheating, lay the cake pan in the "Zone 2" basket.
21. Slide the basket into the Air Fryer and press "Time" to adjust for 25 minutes.

22. After cooking time is finished, press "Start/Pause" to stop cooking.
23. Take out both pans from the Air Fryer.
24. Place the pans onto a counter to cool.
25. After 10 minutes, turn the rum cake onto a wire rack to cool thoroughly before cutting.
26. Let the cheesecake cool thoroughly.
27. Then, move it into your refrigerator to chill before enjoying it.
28. Just before enjoying, dust with the powdered sugar.
29. Spread the jam on top and enjoy.

Conversion Charts

Mass

Imperial (ounces)	Metric (gram)
¼ ounce	7 grams
½ ounce	14 grams
1 ounce	28 grams
2 ounces	56 grams
3 ounces	85 grams
4 ounces	113 grams
5 ounces	141 grams
6 ounces	150 grams
7 ounces	198 grams
8 ounces	226 grams
9 ounces	255 grams
10 ounces	283 grams
11 ounces	311 grams
12 ounces	340 grams
13 ounces	368 grams
14 ounces	396 grams
15 ounces	425 grams
16 ounces/ 1 pound	455 grams

Cups & Spoon

Cups	Metric
¼ cup	60 milliliters
1/3 cup	80 milliliters
½ cup	120 milliliters
1 cup	240 milliliters
Spoon	**Metric**
¼ teaspoon	1¼ milliliters
½ teaspoon	2½ milliliters
1 teaspoon	5 milliliters
2 teaspoons	10 milliliters
1 tablespoon	20 milliliters

Liquid

Imperial	Metric
1 fluid ounce	30 milliliters
2 fluid ounces	60 milliliters
3½ fluid ounces	80 milliliters
2¾ fluid ounces	100 milliliters
4 fluid ounces	125 milliliters
5 fluid ounces	150 milliliters
6 fluid ounces	180 milliliters
7 fluid ounces	200 milliliters
8¾ fluid ounces	250 milliliters
10½ fluid ounces	310 milliliters
13 fluid ounces	375 milliliters
15 fluid ounces	430 milliliters
16 fluid ounces	475 milliliters
17 fluid ounces	500 milliliters
21½ fluid ounces	625 milliliters
26 fluid ounces	750 milliliters
35 fluid ounces	1 Liter
44 fluid ounces	1¼ Liters
52 fluid ounces	1½ Liters
70 fluid ounces	2 Liters
88 fluid ounces	2½ Liters

Temperature

Fahrenheit (°F)	Celsius (°C)
275°F	140°C
300°F	150°C
325°F	165°C
350°F	177°C
375°F	190°C
400°F	200°C
425°F	220°C
450°F	230°C
450°F	230°C
475°F	245°C
500°F	260°C

Conclusion

The 2-Basket Air Fryer has emerged as a game-changer in modern culinary innovation, offering enthusiasts a remarkable avenue to explore their gastronomic creativity. Its dual-basket design not only doubles the capacity for culinary experiments but also introduces a new level of efficiency in cooking. With its ability to simultaneously prepare diverse dishes, the 2-Basket Air Fryer redefines multitasking in the kitchen, catering to the demands of contemporary lifestyles where time and space are often limited resources. This appliance embraces convenience and promotes healthier cooking choices by drastically reducing the need for oil, resulting in delectable and nourishing meals.

In crafting the 2-Basket Air Fryer Cookbook, the true essence of this culinary marvel has been captured. The cookbook stands as a testament to the versatile potential of the appliance, offering a curated collection of recipes that span cuisines, dietary preferences, and meal occasions. From crispy appetizers to mouthwatering mains and even delightful desserts, the cookbook demonstrates the breadth of culinary exploration the 2-Basket Air Fryer enables. As the pages unfold, it becomes evident that this cookbook is not merely a compilation of recipes but a guide that empowers cooks to embrace the convenience, health benefits, and creative possibilities that the 2-Basket Air Fryer brings to the kitchen. With user-friendly instructions and inspiring culinary ideas, the cookbook is an indispensable companion, inspiring beginners, and seasoned chefs to embark on a flavorful journey that seamlessly marries innovation with taste.

Made in the USA
Las Vegas, NV
02 August 2024

93304851R00046